TEACHING SCIENCE
With Interactive
Notebooks

Kellie Marcarelli
Foreword by Rodger W. Bybee

CORWIN
A SAGE Company

For information:

Corwin
A SAGE Company
2455 Teller Road
Thousand Oaks, California 91320
(800) 233-9936
Fax: (800) 417-2466
www.corwin.com

SAGE Ltd.
1 Oliver's Yard
55 City Road
London EC1Y 1SP
United Kingdom

SAGE India Pvt. Ltd.
B 1/I 1 Mohan Cooperative Industrial Area
Mathura Road, New Delhi 110 044
India

SAGE Asia-Pacific Pte. Ltd.
33 Pekin Street #02-01
Far East Square
Singapore 048763

Printed in the United States of America.

Library of Congress Cataloging-in-Publication Data

Marcarelli, Kellie.
Teaching science with interactive notebooks / Kellie Marcarelli.
    p. cm.
Includes bibliographical references and index.
ISBN 978-1-4129-5403-7 (pbk.)
    1. Science—Study and teaching. 2. School notebooks. I. Title.

Q181.M1753 2010
507.1—dc22   2010009984

This book is printed on acid-free paper.

14 15 16 17 10 9 8 7

Acquisitions Editor:	Cathy Hernandez
Editorial Assistant:	Sarah Bartlett
Production Editor:	Cassandra Margaret Seibel
Copy Editor:	Adam Dunham
Typesetter:	C&M Digitals (P) Ltd.
Proofreader:	Susan Schon
Indexer:	Sheila Bodell
Cover Designer:	Scott Van Atta

TEACHING SCIENCE
With Interactive Notebooks

Contents

Additional materials and resources related to
Teaching Science With Interactive Notebooks can be
found at http://www.corwin.com/teachingscience.

Foreword

Like many teachers, I was left on my own when I began teaching ninth-grade earth science in junior high school. In my excitement to do well, I looked for activities and strategies that would help my students learn science. My method of teaching science courses provided some fundamentals, and the textbook helped. But, student motivations and interest emerged as an issue when I had my own classroom. It would have been great to have suggestions that would help me improve. Well, now there is just such a resource.

Kellie Marcarelli's *Teaching Science With Interactive Notebooks* provides teacher-friendly, practical strategies that all science teachers can use. Kellie's writing conveys her enthusiasm for teaching her students science. Reading the book is like having a professional discussion with a colleague and having that individual describe practical strategies and methods.

The use of interactive notebooks in science classes is deceptively simple yet profoundly rich in the many ways it can enhance student learning. Let me give some examples. In this age of accountability, science teachers try to find ways to develop literacy skills such as writing—interactive notebooks in science will complement this. Teachers search for ways to incorporate learning outcomes related to scientific inquiry—interactive notebooks do this. Science teachers look for opportunities that will help students develop some of the skills needed in a 21st century workforce—and interactive notebooks do this.

I was impressed with something else Ms. Marcarelli did in her book. She cited research that supported many of her strategies and recommendations. She conveyed her odyssey of searching for new and better ways to help students learn only to find that researchers have confirmed her discoveries. Her discussions and explorations provide an excellent model for all science teachers.

The book is rich with examples and illustrations. All are well placed, appropriate, and elaborate the points being made in the text. I encourage you to slow down and look carefully at the examples. They are a wonderful complement to the text.

I cannot resist mentioning one other feature of this book. Kellie aligns her instruction and her use of notebooks with the BSCS 5E Instructional Model. Ms. Marcarelli walks the talk of implementing useful, research-based ways to integrate a variety of instructional strategies.

I am honored that Kellie Marcarelli asked me to write a brief foreword to her book. I found reviewing the book and preparing this foreword an insightful conversation with a colleague. Her enthusiasm for science and students, her understanding of teaching and learning, and her communication with teachers are all wonderful features of *Teaching Science With Interactive Notebooks.* You should read and use this book!

Rodger W. Bybee
Executive Director (Emeritus)
BSCS

Preface

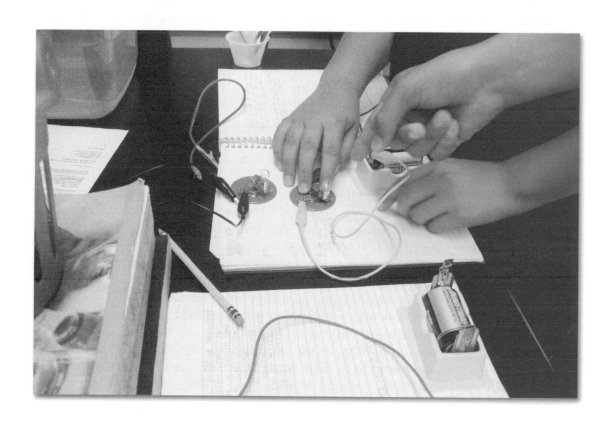

An interactive science notebook is a highly beneficial learning tool that develops students' communication skills, cognitive organization skills, and sense of responsibility for their own learning. The idea behind interactive notebooks is to engage students in collaborative inquiry as a way of learning science content. Using the notebooks, students record their observations, ideas, and thinking, and they reflect on their learning in a variety of interactive ways. In addition, students can use the interactive notebooks to self-assess their work while gaining interdisciplinary skills and making connections across subject areas.

Students' own feelings about the benefits of using their interactive notebooks are telling. Abdullah, an eighth grader, wrote, "For me, the notebook shows a progression over the year and organizes all my thoughts and data into one place. This way it is much easier to compare results and correct errors." Nils, also an eighth grader, said, "My notebook allows me to show what I think. Being able to draw out and describe what I am thinking allows me to more vividly express my thoughts or opinions."

Students enjoy the freedom to express ideas learned from the curriculum in a way that is unique and makes meaning for them. Teachers use interactive notebooks to better understand where a student is coming from, what he or she is thinking, and what drives that thinking.

I have been using interactive notebooks in my middle-school science classroom for more than 14 years. I originally developed the idea for using interactive notebooks after attending an Advancement Via Individual Determination (AVID) conference and have been modifying their use with my students ever since. I am passionate about the use of interactive notebooks because I have seen how they can be powerful tools to increase student learning. Using interactive notebooks has changed my practice, and I have become a strong advocate for their use.

In this book, I explain how interactive notebooks work in my classroom. My goal is to provide a guide for science educators who want to use interactive notebooks with their students in order to enhance the learning experience. I also hope to offer new strategies to teachers who have been using interactive notebooks and want to take their students' notebooking to new levels.

HOW THIS BOOK IS ARRANGED

Chapter 1 provides an introduction to the use of interactive notebooks in the classroom. I explain how notebooks are used, discuss the benefits of using notebooks, and examine what research shows about using notebooks.

Chapter 2 looks at how the organization of notebooks promotes learning. Here, I unpack the unique features that make the use of interactive notebooks more effective than the use of conventional notebooks in the science classroom.

Chapter 3 offers guidance for promoting students' buy in and ownership of their interactive notebooks.

Chapter 4 shows how interactive notebooks are used in the classroom for both teacher-guided work as well as student-generated work. This chapter includes a discussion of metacognitive thought processes and examples of student learning and understanding.

Chapters 5 and 6 describe the nuts and bolts of implementing interactive notebooks in the classroom. These chapters provide in-depth guidance for execution, time management, and grading the notebooks.

Chapter 7 emphasizes the importance of writing in science, provides strategies for modeling writing, and includes student examples. This chapter also introduces protocols for engaging students in self-reflective writing and thesis papers to solidify, extend, and express their learning. Chapter 7 also explores strategies for assessing student work.

Chapter 8 explores strategies to encourage students to talk and discusses the importance of collaborating with peers in order to expand their knowledge of scientific concepts.

Chapter 9 concludes the book with a review of the benefits of interactive notebooks.

SPECIAL FEATURES

There are numerous examples of actual student work as well as checklists, time-management tips, and more. Reproducible pages are included in the Resources section at the end of this book.

WHO THIS BOOK IS FOR

This book is designed as a tool for science educators who are interested in improving student content and process skills while promoting student engagement and understanding. Although I am a middle school teacher, other teachers have used this model successfully with elementary and high school students. Novice teachers have embraced these techniques and also experienced success. The book is designed as a working resource for teachers, just as interactive notebooks are a working resource for students. I encourage you to fill this book with your own ideas on sticky notes or in the margins, your reflections, highlighted key ideas, and taped-in student work samples.

NEXT STEPS

Throughout this book, I share my processes and offer tips about what worked for me. Of course, you should feel free to adapt these ideas to meet the needs of your own students and teaching situation. I encourage you to read and reflect upon the processes and ideas in this book and then just do it—get your interactive notebooks up and running. Although the process I describe begins with a new school year, you certainly don't need to wait for a new school year to start. Any new science unit provides the perfect opportunity to begin using interactive science notebooks and harnessing their power as a learning tool.

Acknowledgments

The inspiration for this book came from amazing students and the discoveries they make each day in the classroom, along with the equally amazing teachers who get to be witness to these miracles when they happen in class. I am grateful for the students I have had the pleasure to teach throughout the years, especially those who attended Pershing and Challenger Middle Schools in San Diego Unified School District. Victoria and Howard Nguyen, Ana Segovia, Valeria Rosas, Tori Maches, and Sara Shah, your awesome notebooks are works of art, filled with deep thinking and profound connections. Thank you for sharing your work with anyone who reads this book. To the inspirational teachers that I have had the pleasure of working with, thank you for sharing your vision, experience, collaboration, and love for teaching.

To the mentors and advisors in my community, who have taught me so much about everything from leading to teaching, especially, Kim Bess, Don Whisman, Kathy DiRanna, Rodger Bybee, Joseph A. Taylor, Nancy Taylor, Janet Powell, Nancy Landes, Jim Short, Bob Hamm, Geoff Martin, Sarah Sullivan, Sheelagh Moran, Sam Wong, and Penney. Thank you for believing in me and providing an opportunity for me to continually grow.

For revising my work and helping me to think critically, I thank Susan Benson, Jeremiah Potter, Aaron Rubin, Rick Budzynski, Heather Nellis, Carleen Hemric, Felicia Ryder, Kerry Yates, Jean Ward, Frank Calantropio, and Anna Lubatti. You have all made a profound difference!

Finally, for their continued support throughout this grueling process, Ralph, Marissa, Nana, Erica, John, Dolly, Dad, Anna, Alex, D., Jamie, Lisa, Ricky, Rachael, Lauren, Randy, Ree, Don, Sonia, Frank, Kendall, Ken, Joan, Melisa, Don B., Kiera, Lee, Lisa, Angelina, Dylan, Maureen, Kay, Lina, Joey, Michelle, Joanne, Joseph, Sebastion, Nicole Buchanan, Lance Justice, Kim Luttgen, Tammy Moriarty, Rick Barr, Dan Grendziak, Terry Allinger, Daniel Cook, Princess Rostrata, Gerald Gapusan, Andrea Pfaff, Kathleen Blair, Scott Hillier, Jim Rohr, John Yochelson, Jack Annala, Kathy Jones, Michael Harris, Jackie Gallaway, Jennifer Weibert, Panera Bread Company—for allowing me sit in their restaurant and write for hours—and Linda Lotze (who didn't tattle on me when I ditched school to finish this book).

Special thanks to San Diego Unified School District; San Diego County Office of Education; K–12 Alliance; WestEd; the authors of *Interactions in Physical Science*, especially Sharon Bendall and Fred Goldberg; AVID, and BSCS (Biological Sciences and Curriculum Study). Thanks to Jean Ward for editing my manuscript and helping me get a contract with Corwin. Thank you, Corwin, for all your support throughout the process, especially Cathy Hernandez, managing editor.

Disclaimer: My brain has gone to mush, and I would like to apologize in advance for not mentioning any person I am forgetting to mention. Whoever you are, you were fabulous, and I will probably remember you after the acknowledgments have long been sent to the editor.

PUBLISHER'S ACKNOWLEDGMENTS

Corwin gratefully acknowledges the contributions of the following individuals:

Michael Baker, Eighth-Grade Science Teacher
Memorial Middle School
Albany, OR

John Burns, Middle School Science Teacher
Visiting Lecturer, Department of Education
California State Polytechnic University, Pomona
Pomona, CA

Cindy Corlett, Eighth-Grade Science Teacher
Cimarron Middle School
Parker, CO

Steve DeAngelis, Middle School Science Teacher
Marancook Community School
Readfield, ME

Hubert Dyasi, Professor Emeritus, Science Education
City College of New York
Yonkers, NY

Susan Harmon, Technology/FACS Science Teacher
Neodesha Junior/Senior High School
Neodesha, KS

Jane Hunn, Middle School Science Teacher
Tippecanoe Valley Middle School
Akron, IN

Sally Koczan, Science Teacher
Meramec Elementary School
Clayton, MO

Deb Las, Middle School Science Teacher
John Adams Middle School
Rochester, MN

Susan Leeds, Teacher/Science Curriculum Leader
Howard Middle School
Winter Park, FL

Maria Mesires, Seventh-Grade Science Teacher
Case Middle School
Watertown, NY

Jeanine Nakakura, Gifted and Talented Resource Teacher
Aiea, HI

Judith Onslow, Middle School Science Teacher
Girdwood Elementary/Junior High School
Girdwood, AK

Charre Todd, Middle School Science Teacher
Norman Junior High School
Crossett, AR

About the Author

 **Kellie Marcarelli** is a middle school science teacher and department chair at Pershing Middle School in the San Diego Unified School District, where she teaches eighth grade physics and chemistry. Beyond the classroom, Kellie serves as a trainer, teacher-leader, and curriculum evaluator and assists in the screening process for the Greater San Diego Science and Engineering Fair. Her professional experience includes working as a staff developer for the Middle School Science Education Leadership Initiative (MSSELI), the California Math and Science Partnership program, and the San Diego Unified School District; presenting regularly at NSTA's national conference as well as state and regional science education conferences, and working with WestEd's K–12 Alliance. She is also actively involved in STEM outreach with local professionals in the science community. She is the recipient of the California State Science Fair Teacher of the Year, the San Diego Science Alliance Partnership Teacher of the Year, and the Greater San Diego Science and Engineering Fair Teacher of the Year awards.

Kellie's passion for using interactive notebooks in the science classroom grew out of her desire to improve student learning and to provide students with a method for organizing their metacognitive thoughts. She believes that the students are scientists, therefore they should act like scientists and document their findings and ideas. Kellie lives in San Diego with her daughter, Marissa . . . and loves the color red!

1

Introduction

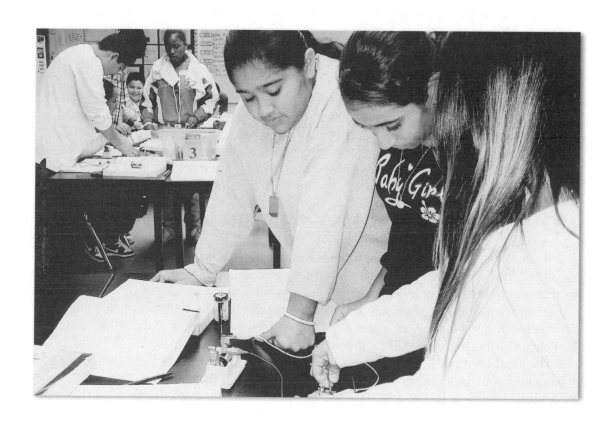

WHAT IS AN INTERACTIVE NOTEBOOK?

An interactive notebook is a tool students use to make connections prior to new learning, to revise their thinking, and to deepen their understandings of the world around them. It is the culmination of a student's work throughout the year that shows both the content learned (input) and the reflective knowledge (output) gained. Put another way, an interactive notebook provides a space where students may take what is inside their brains, lay it out, make meaning, apply it, and share it with their peers, parents, and teachers. I use the term *interactive* to describe how these notebooks can be used. That is to say, the notebooks support interactivity and an exchange of ideas from teacher to student, student to student, student to parent, and parent to teacher.

Here's what one student wrote about her interactive notebook:

> It's like my own piece of property that I have to take responsibility for. It shows my personal thinking and creativity. My notebook shows that I can think for myself and figure out where I went wrong for myself instead of someone telling me. I like my interactive notebook because I feel like it's my own little book where I can write my own questions and answer them. However, I think it represents me. Like if I were to look through a stranger's interactive notebook, I would get a sense of their personality, too—cool.

Teachers use interactive notebooks to increase student thinking and achievement. They provide a means of communicating, tracking, assessing, and reflecting the work students do. Interactive notebooks provide a window into the minds of students to reveal their true understanding and their misconceptions, and they provide an opportunity for teachers to open up new horizons for their students to explore.

HOW ARE INTERACTIVE NOTEBOOKS USED?

Below is a brief overview of the process of using notebooks as part of the science curriculum. In the chapters that follow, we will examine the steps of using interactive notebooks in much greater detail.

At the beginning of each science unit, the teacher works with the class to develop an overarching question or problem that will be researched during the unit. All learning during the unit will be linked back to this question.

The unit continues with several lab investigations. The teacher starts each one with a key question, giving students time to write what they think in their notebooks and then discuss it in groups. The teacher and students explore the ideas in class, and students individually form their hypotheses. This allows students to start thinking about the topic and prepares students for the next step.

Students then participate in an inquiry-based investigation—gathering data, observing, forming questions, making sketches, and beginning to formulate ideas about the topic being studied. Student interaction and probing questions by the teacher and peers are essential parts of the process. Students record the processes and data in their notebooks.

After the investigation is over, the students and teacher come together as a class for a discussion (I call this "an accountable talk" session), where the collected data is used to make meaning of student's initial ideas and questions. This is the exciting part of the process. Discussions may become heated as students' ideas are challenged.

The evidence that was gathered during the lab drives the entire conversation, and some students hold on to their beliefs, while other students change theirs. Sometimes, students discuss the idea that the data might be flawed because of too many variables. For example, during one discussion, two students debated the idea that the tests performed on various gasses produced minimal results because the method that some groups used to gather the gas was crude. The conversation went on for over 30 minutes, until the class came to the conclusion that as long as they noted whether the gas burned or not it was fine because no exact numbers were being applied to the final conclusion.

A homework assignment completes the processing. Using their notebooks, students write conclusions or summaries, create graphs, or complete other similar assignments designed to push their thinking to the next level.

On subsequent days, students complete additional investigations, using their notebooks and following this same process. Students become accustomed to and comfortable with a process that starts with a question, introduces ideas through lab or other inquiry experience, includes hypothesizing, collection of data, presentation of evidence, and summarization. Keeping this lesson framework constant, with variation in the learning experiences to keep interest high, this scientific method for investigation becomes the continuing mode through which to explore any new ideas in class. The process, patterns, and expectations remain the same. By following an established protocol that stays constant, the student has the teacher's format to rely on every day and every lesson.

WHAT ARE THE BENEFITS OF USING INTERACTIVE NOTEBOOKS?

The benefits of using interactive notebooks can be considered from three vantage points: developing students' thinking in ways that prepare them to be part of the 21st-century workforce, increasing communication between stakeholders, and differentiating instruction.

Preparing Students to Compete Globally

On the Third International Mathematics and Science Study, U.S. students performed poorly compared to their counterparts in other countries. These results have fueled an increased sense of urgency in regard to improving science instruction in U.S. schools. According to Wallis (2006), schools can better prepare students for the future by

- Starting earlier in the student's developmental stage;
- Monitoring the gap between minority and majority social classes;
- Providing opportunity to challenge students, to push them further;
- Using computers to support instructional goals rather than just to be using them;
- Providing inquiry lessons that bridge relevant content; and
- Involving the community.

Using interactive notebooks in the classroom targets all of the aforementioned needs and helps develop the globally competitive student. Notebooks address these needs by

- Connecting students' thinking and experiences with science concepts;
- Engaging students in collaborative inquiry as a way of learning science content;

- Providing opportunities for all students;
- Creating a concrete record of reflection, assessment, and connections that can be viewed and discussed;
- Developing academic language; and
- Providing students with an opportunity to think critically and make informed decisions.

The interactive notebook becomes real evidence of student learning and thinking, a shaping tool for future productive citizens in the science world.

Increasing Communication Between Stakeholders

Notebooking promotes communication between the stakeholders—students, teachers, and parents. A science classroom exposes students to shared experiences of observable marvels or happenings. The interactive notebook is a way of capturing these common experiences on paper, in a place where it won't get lost, so that students can refer back to the common experiences whenever they need them as a way of driving discourse. This provides students with an opportunity to come to consensus and build on the knowledge that was collaboratively gained.

Consider an example based on Newton's first law of motion. As part of their inquiry, students observed low-friction cars at rest and at a constant speed moving in the same direction. They observed the interactions and collected data (input). Figure 1.1 shows an example of student observations. Students used their findings as evidence to support their ideas about the phenomena (output). The interactive notebooks provided a means of communicating with the teacher. The teacher read the students' work and gained an understanding of their thinking processes. Student entries become evidence not only of what they know but also of how they know it. Entries also indicated what students don't know.

The interactive notebook also enhances communication between the student and the parent or the teacher and the parent. Parents can simply pick up the interactive notebook and start asking questions about the student's entries. The interactive notebook provides parents with evidence of a student's conceptual understanding and personal reflections. A notebook rubric, which is permanently affixed in the front of the notebook, can be used by parents, teachers, and students to discuss expectations and the extent to which the student is meeting them.

Differentiating Instruction to Meet the Needs of All Students

When working with English language learners or students with special needs, the interactive notebook is an effective tool for the development and reinforcement of scientific or academic language. The notebook provides a safe place to practice writing and express prior knowledge and newly acquired knowledge. The interactive notebooks can be reviewed at meetings with intervention teachers and language specialists to provide evidence about how students are developing in your science class. It can help facilitate the development of intervention strategies for students with special needs.

Figure 1.1   By looking at this sample of a student's observations, one can see that the lab experiment helped guide the student to his final concluding ideas. His use of diagrams is helpful to the teacher because they show what he observed, and they make it easy to follow his thinking process. The diagrams become evidence for his final ideas. In those concluding ideas, he sums up Newton's first law.

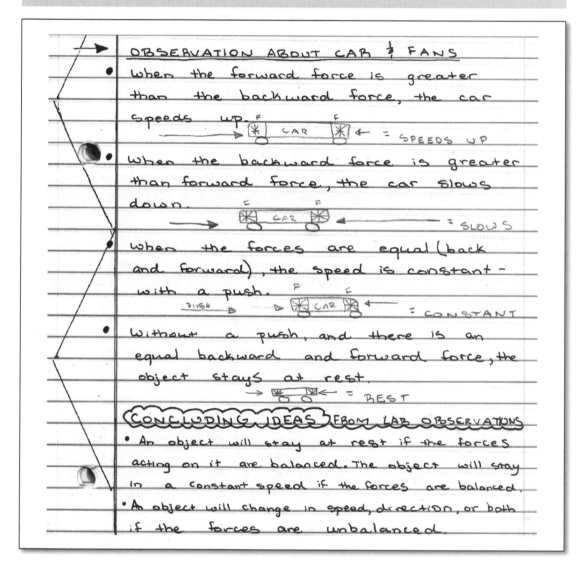

WHAT RESEARCH SUPPORTS USING INTERACTIVE NOTEBOOKS?

Notebooks support effective science instruction in a multitude of ways. According to *How Students Learn: Science in the Classroom* (Donovan & Bransford, 2005) science instruction should

- Elicit and address students' prior conceptions of scientific phenomena;
- Help students build deep understandings of science subject matter and of scientific inquiry (i.e., what it means to "do science"); and
- Help students monitor and take control of their own learning (metacognition).

Thoughtful use of interactive science notebooks can help meet all three of these recommendations. The interactive science notebook allows students the opportunity to identify their preexisting ideas, deepen and refine their scientific ideas throughout the learning activities, and reflect on their learning.

Beyond the connection to the general findings of Donovan and Bransford (2005) about effective science instruction, researchers have found specific evidence of how interactive notebooks promote student learning and increase achievement.

- Science notebooks expose students' thinking, providing important insights about student understandings and serving as formative assessment tools (Hargrove & Nesbit, 2003; Gilbert & Kotelman, 2005).
- Notebooks encourage active learning and provide opportunities for students to pursue their own interests and tackle authentic problems (Hargrove & Nesbit, 2003; Gilbert & Kotelman, 2005).
- Notebooks offer numerous opportunities to develop and enhance students' writing skills (Gilbert & Kotelman, 2005; Young, 2003).
- Notebooks provide a structure and support for differentiated learning, helping all students to achieve (Amaral, Garrison, & Klentschy, 2002; Gilbert & Kotelman, 2005).
- Interactive notebooks help improve students' organizational skills (Madden, 2001).
- Notebooks facilitate communication with parents and can be used to provide them with evidence of student growth (Hargrove & Nesbit, 2003; Young, 2003).

Some of the research on the use of notebooks focused directly on students' understanding of "doing science" and the nature of science and found that

- Thoughtfully implemented science notebooks use reflective writing and include a think-aloud feature that is common to the notebooks of actual scientists as they explore the world in a first hand manner (Magnusson & Palincsar, 2003);
- Science notebooks engage students in authentic science processes, such as recording information and data and engaging in research, collaboration, and analysis (Hargrove & Nesbit, 2003; Young, 2003); and
- Using an interactive notebook allows a student to think, record data and observations, and reflect just as professional scientists do (Young, 2003).

A CLOSER LOOK AT HOW NOTEBOOKS SUPPORT EFFECTIVE INSTRUCTION

We can consider notebooking from another vantage point—by examining how the processes of notebooking correlate with the nine effective strategies identified by Marzano, Pickering, and Pollock (2001) in *Classroom Instruction That Works*. Figure 1.2 shows how these strategies are integral to interactive-notebooking processes.

Figure 1.2   Interactive Notebooks and Effective Instructional Strategies

Strategies Described in *Classroom Instruction That Works*	Interactive Science Notebooks
Identifying similarities and differences	Notebooks are used by students to record their observations and make connections between concepts.
Summarizing and note taking	Students take notes as they complete science investigations and write summaries during each unit.
Reinforcing effort and providing recognition	Notebooks provide an ongoing record of student work and growth, leading to recognition from their peers, teachers, and parents.
Homework and practice	Homework assignments and practice are built into the use of interactive notebooks, providing valuable processing opportunities.
Nonlinguistic representations	Students illustrate their observations during each inquiry-based lab activity and create different kinds of graphs to represent their data.
Cooperative learning	Students work with partners and in teams to complete investigations and engage in classroom discourse.
Setting objectives and providing feedback	Students help identify key questions to explore during each unit. Notebooks allow the teacher to provide continual, specific feedback.
Generating and testing hypotheses	Students build the habit of generating hypotheses before beginning their explorations.
Questions, cues, and advance organizers	Questions are present throughout students' interactive notebooks, and the notebooks are richly littered with graphic organizers.

The following examples of student work show how interactive science notebooks incorporate many effective instructional strategies.

Identifying Similarities and Differences

Figure 1.3 This is an excellent example of the differences between a series and parallel circuit. As an educator, it is clear to me that the student understands the concept of how each works. Again, look at the use of arrows which provide information about her understanding not only of how each circuit works, but also how the energy flows and in which direction.

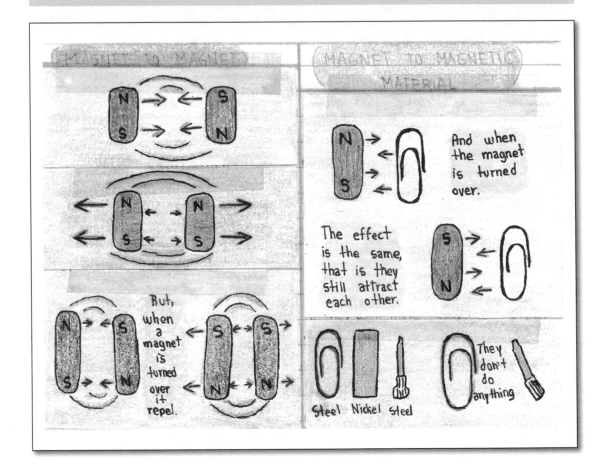

Figure 1.4 This is a graphic that a student created to show her understanding of the similarities and differences between magnetic interactions and electric charge interactions.

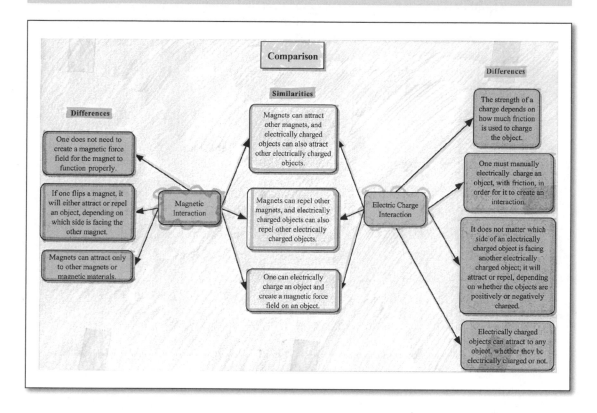

Summarizing and Note Taking

Figure 1.5   Under "Observations," the student recorded pieces of information that she can use later to formulate or back up claims. She was experimenting with a wooden puck connected to a balloon to see how forces affect motion. Her comments that "The balloon slowly got smaller decreasing in speed while gliding on a cushion of air" and "The puck slowed down because it sometimes just floated in place unless you pushed it" can be used later as evidence to prove that forces affect motion.

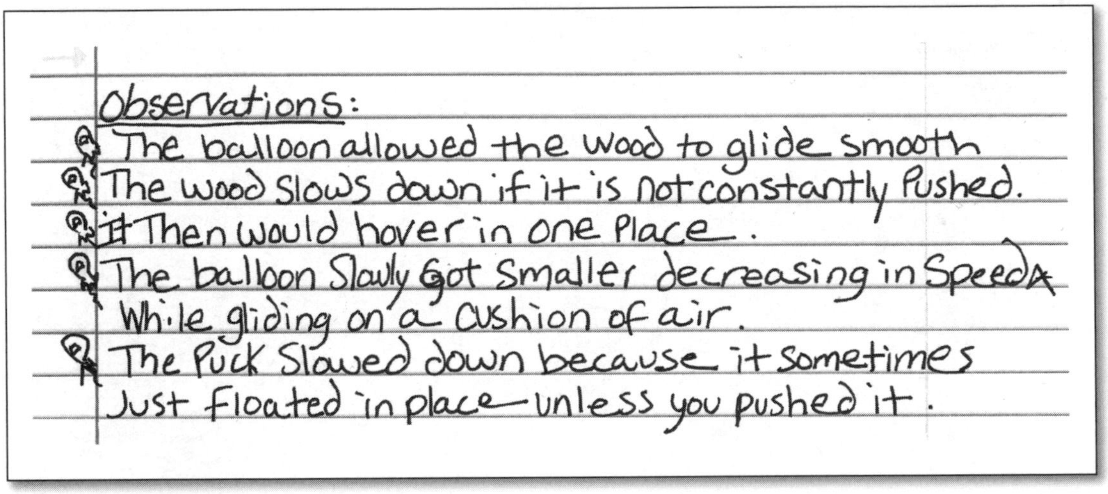

Observations:
- The balloon allowed the wood to glide smooth
- The wood slows down if it is not constantly pushed.
- It Then would hover in one place.
- The balloon slowly got smaller decreasing in speed while gliding on a cushion of air.
- The Puck slowed down because it sometimes just floated in place unless you pushed it.

Figure 1.6   Under "Throughout Observations," the student wrote specifics about mass and how it decreased, then she self-corrected by writing that the mass should have remained the same both before and after. The final bullet is a starting point for her claim, "In a closed system interactions do not change their mass," which answers the question, "In a closed system, does the mass increase, decrease, or stay the same?"

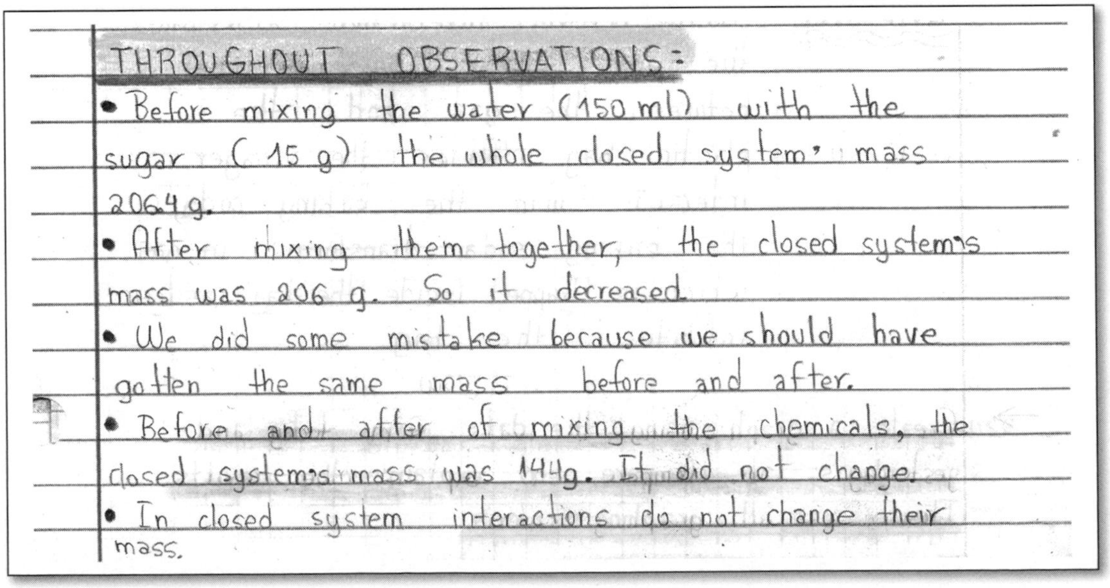

THROUGHOUT   OBSERVATIONS:
- Before mixing the water (150 ml) with the sugar (15 g) the whole closed system: mass 206.4 g.
- After mixing them together, the closed system's mass was 206 g. So it decreased
- We did some mistake because we should have gotten the same mass before and after.
- Before and after of mixing the chemicals, the closed system's mass was 144g. It did not change.
- In closed system interactions do not change their mass.

Homework and Practice

Figure 1.7   For this homework assignment, I asked students to observe an interaction at home and create an energy diagram. At the bottom of the page, I asked for a parent signature, which serves two purposes: one, to make the parent check the homework; and two, to force a conversation between the parent and student. This gave the student an opportunity to reinforce what he learned in class by having to explain and teach the idea to his parent.

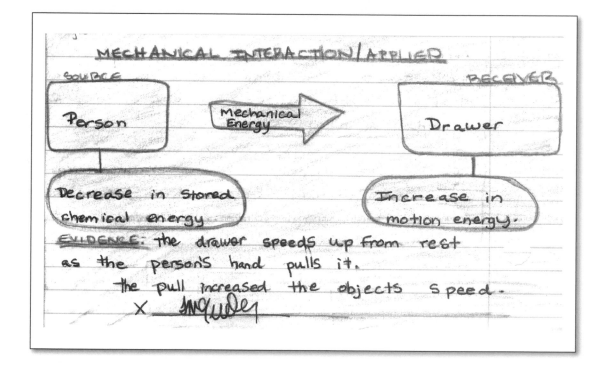

Nonlinguistic Representations

Figure 1.8 This student shows her understanding of an interaction by drawing butter in a pan before and after it melts. The arrows point to the object that changes state, and the drawing shows the butter changing shape.

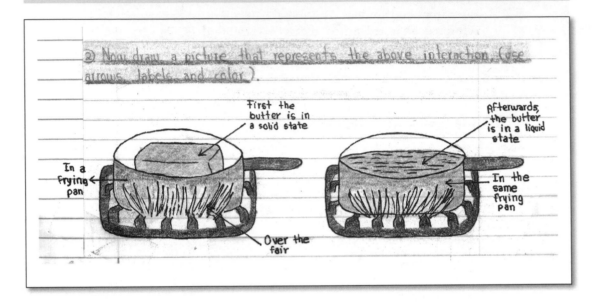

Figure 1.9   The student shows her understanding of how magnets interact, and you can clearly see from the use of arrows that she understands how magnets interact on both the north and south poles. The student even draws the force field that shows the relationship to energy, revealing a deeper understanding of the interaction between the two. This is the work of a student for whom English is a second language, so the nonlinguistic representations are keys to understanding her thinking processes.

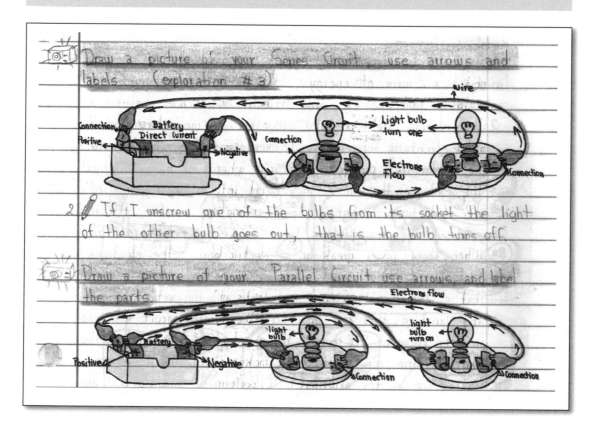

Generating and Testing Hypotheses

Figure 1.10   This is an example of a hypothesis.

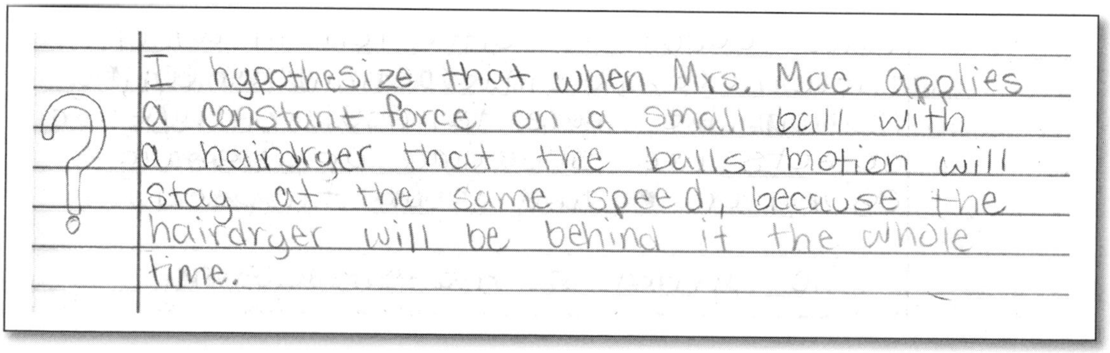

Figure 1.11   This notebook sample shows a student's thinking from beginning to end in the development of a science-fair project that spans six months. She came up with a testable question and through research developed a final hypothesis. You can see the development clearly as you read through to her final hypothesis.

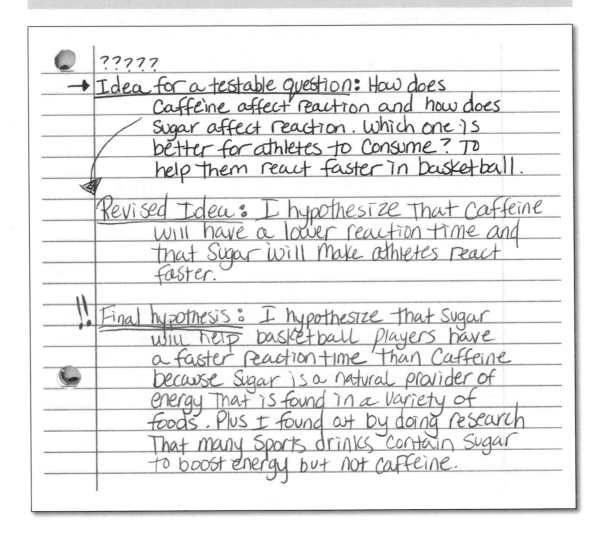

?????

Idea for a testable question: How does caffeine affect reaction and how does sugar affect reaction. Which one is better for athletes to consume? To help them react faster in basketball.

Revised Idea: I hypothesize that caffeine will have a lower reaction time and that sugar will make athletes react faster.

Final hypothesis: I hypothesize that sugar will help basketball players have a faster reaction time than caffeine because sugar is a natural provider of energy that is found in a variety of foods. Plus I found out by doing research that many sports drinks contain sugar to boost energy but not caffeine.

Questions, Cues, and Advance Organizers

Figure 1.12   This student uses a T-chart as a way of sorting and organizing her thoughts.

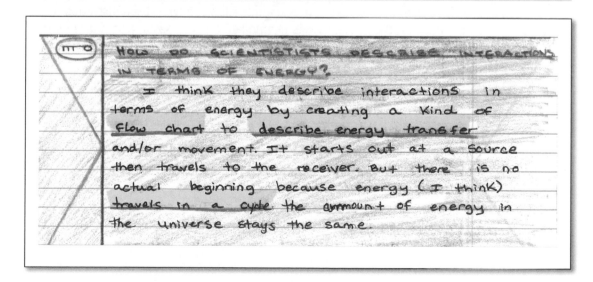

Magnets	Electric Circuits
Attract and Repel	Source of Energy
Polarity	Conductors
Magnetic Material	Insulators
Positive and Negative	Charge, Electric Current
Magnet to Magnet	Hoop-up Wires, Batteries
North and South poles	Series & Parallel, loops
Interactions	Batteries

Brainstorm words related to, or that describe magnets and electric circuits

Figure 1.13   This is an example of a student response to a key question. A key question is a way of tapping into a students' prior knowledge and giving the student a focus point for the day's work. The student knows that there is a source and a receiver, but he is still searching for the "how" part of the concept. Every second page in the interactive notebook begins with a key question, providing plenty of opportunity for students to experience this way of thinking.

HOW DO SCIENTISTS DESCRIBE INTERACTIONS IN TERMS OF ENERGY?

I think they describe interactions in terms of energy by creating a kind of flow chart to describe energy transfer and/or movement. It starts out at a source then travels to the receiver. But there is no actual beginning because energy (I think) travels in a cycle. The ammount of energy in the universe stays the same.

MAKING CONNECTIONS

At the beginning of the year, a class was studying basic electricity concepts. Students investigated the properties of interactions in an open and closed circuit. In their notebooks, they drew, labeled, and explained how these circuits work. They engaged in a series of explorations in which they were trying to make a light turn on, a buzzer sound, and a fan blow air all at the same time. They explored ways to make this happen by using both open and closed circuits. Students inquired, "Why does this one work? Why would it be better to use that one?" These were excellent questions at the time of the lab. But, the real payoff for using notebooks came in March, when students were trying to make meaning of chemistry ideas, and the concept of open and closed systems came up. Because the students had learned to rely on their notebooks to generate conversation, they were able to go back and reference their lab work earlier in the year to inform their conversations.

During an accountable-talk session, one of my students, Jason, said,

An open and closed system is very similar to open and closed circuits because in a closed circuit the energy keeps flowing around and around, keeping the energy in that cycle. In a closed system, nothing can come in or out, it can only move within the system. In an open circuit, the energy can be cut off by a switch that can open and close, allowing energy to flow in or out, making the bulb turn on or shut off. Kind of like an open system that allows mass and volume to increase or decrease because matter can travel in or out of that system.

The conversation continued, and when another student asked for evidence, Jason referenced the data from the lab five months earlier to back up his point. Although Jason was not completely accurate, he was able to use the notebook to identify similarities between the two lab explorations.

From there, the students and I built on Jason's comparison to generate comments about contrast as well as similarity. Other students found differences that also led to a rich discussion. Though the two lab explorations were 5 months apart, the students were able to refer to their earlier learning to construct new understanding. If these students had been completing assignments the traditional way—using loose-leaf paper, or even science materials in packets—the earlier data would have been unavailable, having been discarded and recycled long ago. Because the notebook was maintained all year, Jason had it in front of him, and he used it, which made him feel smart, and helped him draw conclusions around another concept.

Using notebooks helps students come to see learning as integrated. Students rely on the data and become accustomed to asking one another for evidence to back up their thinking. This example also illustrates how interactive notebooks or journals reinforce student effort and provide a way to recognize student work. Jason feels well armed with data and confident enough to speak out to the class with his findings and ideas. His hard work and efforts pay off, and he feels recognized for those efforts, recognized by his teacher and, more important, by his peers.

WHAT YOU NEED TO KNOW TO BEGIN

Like most effective educational practices, incorporating interactive science notebooks into the classroom is a learning process for the teacher. Becoming skilled in their use will not happen overnight for you or your students. The implementation of notebooks takes time in the beginning of the year to set up. You will need to set the parameters and make the expectations very clear for your students from the beginning. Chapters 5 and 6 will go into detail about the first days of school and how to set the stage for notebooking all year.

When thinking about your expectations for interactive notebooks, try to set clear goals that you can sustain all year long. These should be goals you care about and believe are important to overall student learning. For example, if you want students to write in complete sentences, you need to begin holding them accountable for this in September, and continue with the same expectation through the school year to May.

Maintaining successful notebooking throughout the year will take time and effort. It takes patience to work through initial problems. It will be easy to say, "It's not working, so forget it!" I encourage you to start the process, maintain it to the best of your ability, make changes and adjustments where needed, and know that you will do better next year. If you have been using interactive notebooks for a while, challenge yourself to add something new, or focus on a weakness with the goal of increasing student achievement.

Figure 1.14   In my first year using interactive notebooks, I just wanted a place for students to record their work. I wasn't thinking much beyond that. The notebooks that year had little metacognition and were more teacher guided. In the sample below, there is no use of color, the student writes in incomplete sentences, and her work itself doesn't tell me much about what she knows.

OBSERVATION	EVIDENCE
animal – Mrs. Mac is holding it carefully	The box is brown, has tape.
glass thing – holding it carefully	No noises coming from the box.
nothing – she's tricking us	Box is small (shoebox).
marshmallows – we used them before	There aren't any airholes for animals.
dead animal – holding it carefully	I can't see through box.

Figure 1.15   Here is an example of a more recent notebook page. The student uses color, text features, diagrams, and pictures to document what she is learning. An opportunity has been provided to make meaning of the concept; the work is more student-generated, and it shows in-depth understanding of these new ideas.

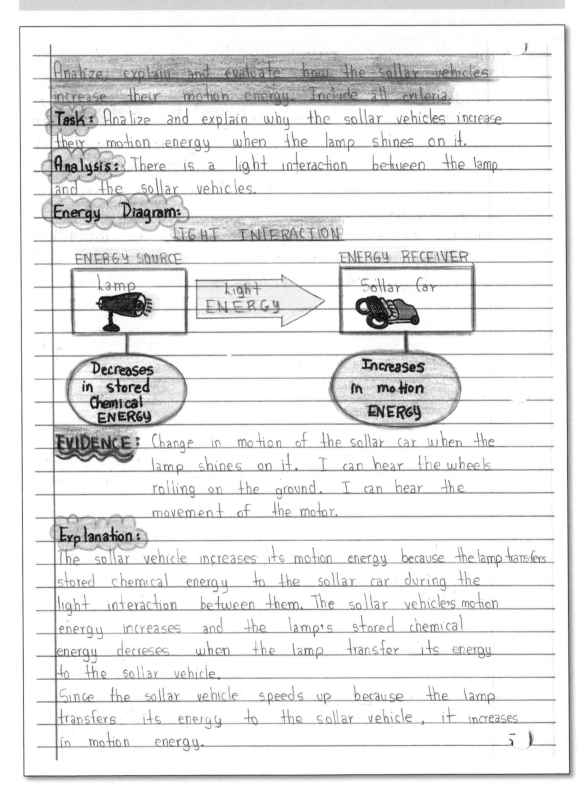

Analize, explain and evaluate how the sollar vehicles increase their motion energy. Include all criteria.

Task: Analize and explain why the sollar vehicles increase their motion energy when the lamp shines on it.

Analysis: There is a light interaction between the lamp and the sollar vehicles.

Energy Diagram:

LIGHT INTERACTION

ENERGY SOURCE   ENERGY RECEIVER

Lamp   Sollar Car

Light ENERGY

Decreases in stored Chemical ENERGY

Increases in motion ENERGY

EVIDENCE: Change in motion of the sollar car when the lamp shines on it. I can hear the wheels rolling on the ground. I can hear the movement of the motor.

Explanation:

The sollar vehicle increases its motion energy because the lamp transfers stored chemical energy to the sollar car during the light interaction between them. The sollar vehicle's motion energy increases and the lamp's stored chemical energy decreses when the lamp transfer its energy to the sollar vehicle.

Since the sollar vehicle speeds up because the lamp transfers its energy to the sollar vehicle, it increases in motion energy.

CLASSROOM SNAPSHOT

What should you see when students use interactive notebooks in your classroom? You should see students constantly using their interactive notebooks! The interactive notebook should be open at all times—during a lab, while using the textbook, and during student discourse.

You should see students writing. The entire interactive notebook is filled with writing from the beginning to the end. Students get the chance to practice writing, revise their writing, complete formal writing, do summary writing, and write conclusions both after labs and for graphs. Writing helps to synthesize student thinking and is used as a way for students to communicate to teachers what they know.

When you open up a notebook, you should see work on every page. You should see the use of text features such as highlighting, color, graphics, headings, and writing. Different parts of each page should jump out at you.

You should see the student work getting progressively better through the notebook pages. You should be able to see the thought process of the students. You should see thoughtful responses with self-reflection embedded in the work; you should see revisions and students adding to previous ideas that were already recorded in their notebook.

The classroom as a whole should be more student driven, with less and less teacher-guided moments as the year advances. Your classroom might be noisy due to the inquiry-type of activities the students are participating in. You might see students talking while using their interactive notebooks as a way of driving discussion. You may hear students using data to back up their claims and making connections to various labs.

You will see students experiencing a high degree of ownership—for their learning and their work. This ownership can provide the teacher opportunities to ask for more out of students, and because they are passionate about their notebooks, students will go the extra mile, which leads to student growth.

You will also see an increase in student discourse. Students will talk in order to clarify ideas, hear new ideas, build on existing ideas, and come to a group consensus about concepts that are introduced in class. Students will use the evidence in their notebooks to back up their statements.

SUMMARY

An interactive notebook is a tool used by teachers to increase student thinking and achievement. Interactive notebooks can be used to track, reflect, communicate, and assess the work students do. They are a record of the work done by students throughout the year. The interactive notebook is a tool of opportunity to help bridge the learning gap. When thinking about implementing the interactive notebook in your classroom, it is helpful to remember to

- Choose a time to begin using interactive notebooks, and just do it!
- Focus on goals and components that are important to you, and stick with them;
- Use interactive notebooks to help students to become better thinkers; and
- Take advantage of their power as tools for interactivity between stakeholders.

Figure 1.16   This is a fabulous example of a *typical* student's notebook page. The focus is on metacognition and explaining through writing what she learned. This example shows the student questioning, self-correcting, diagramming, processing, and understanding friction through pictures and written examples. Notebooking enhanced her individual creative process. Some notebooks become a source of personal pride as "works of art."

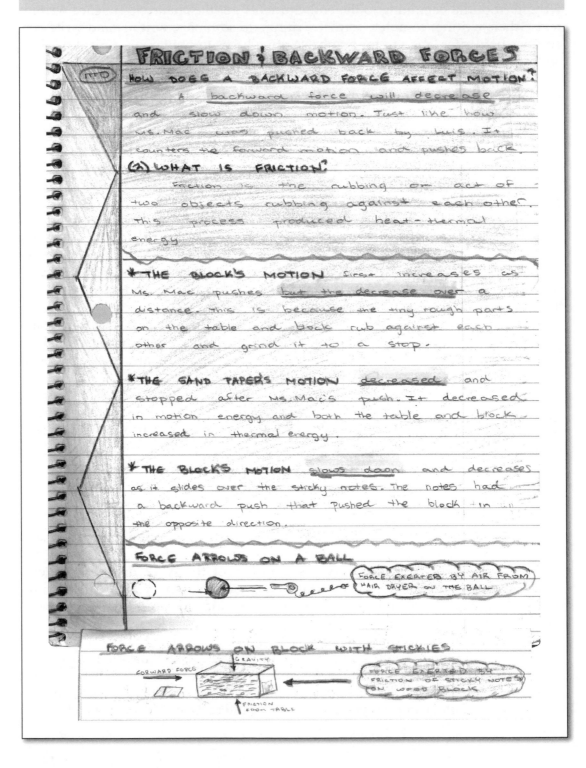

Figure 1.17   This sample shows how students use the notebooks as a way of self-correcting the work they do. This student added to his work after participating in a group discussion about the various types of interactions.

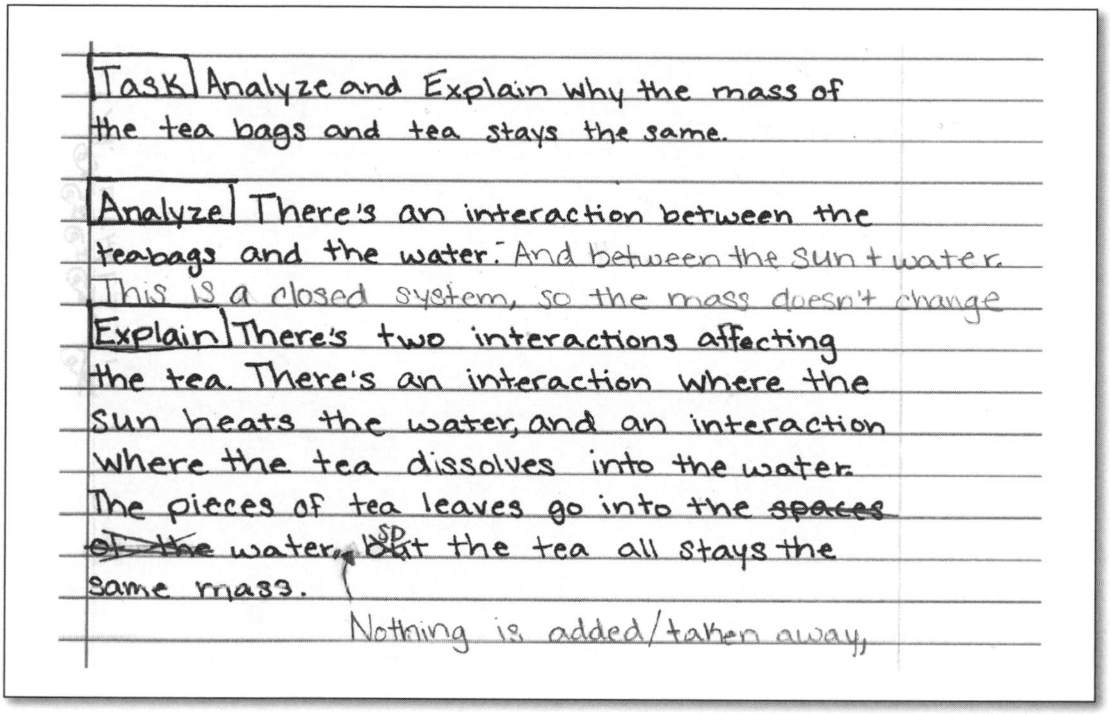

[Task] Analyze and Explain why the mass of the tea bags and tea stays the same.

[Analyze] There's an interaction between the teabags and the water. And between the sun + water. This is a closed system, so the mass doesn't change

[Explain] There's two interactions affecting the tea. There's an interaction where the sun heats the water, and an interaction where the tea dissolves into the water. The pieces of tea leaves go into the ~~spaces of the~~ water, but the tea all stays the same mass.
            Nothing is added/taken away.

2

Organizing Notebooks for Learning

Interactive notebooks are designed to support an inquiry-based approach to science instruction. The organizational structure presented here has been honed and developed through many years of using notebooks with my students and collaborating with my colleagues about how we can deepen student learning. I anticipate that best practices for the use of interactive notebooks will continue to evolve.

THE COMPONENTS OF THE SCIENCE UNIT

The work in interactive notebooks is organized by science units, each of which includes these pages:

- The Unit Cover page. Just as a chapter in a book usually begins on a right-side page, the unit cover page is a recto or right-side page. It includes the unit title and student illustrations.
- The Aha Connections pages. These two pages are a spread and provide a place for students to record the key question and the summary statements about the major concepts they are learning throughout the unit.
- Input and Output pages. The input page and output page are also a spread. Students record observations, data, and results of each investigation on the input (right-side) page. They process this information and express higher-level thinking on the output (left-side) page. Each science unit includes about 10 input-output spreads.
- Self-Reflection page. At the end of the unit, students write a five-paragraph reflective paper about their work during the unit, their own sense of the depth of their learning, their developing science skills, and so on. The reflective paper is affixed to this page in the notebook.
- The Aha Connections Thesis page. For this multiparagraph, formal paper students generate a thesis based on the work done during the unit, providing lines of evidence, and drawing a final conclusion. The formal paper is affixed to this page in the notebook.

> I teach four to five science units each year. Although the exact number varies, if we assume each unit uses about 25 pages, and I complete about five units a year, my students are using 125 pages. Add to this the 8 pages at the front of the notebook and we have a total of 133 pages. This fits perfectly in the 70-sheet notebooks I use, which have 140 pages if you count the front and back sides of each sheet.

NOTEBOOKS AND THE LEARNING CYCLE

My science instruction is modeled on the 5E Learning Cycle (Bybee, 2002); so as I develop science units, I think about everything students will do in terms of the 5Es:

- Engage: The teacher sets the stage for learning by introducing an essential question and using some kind of hook to elicit student interest.
- Explore: Students engage in inquiry, exploring, raising questions, and developing and testing hypotheses.
- Explain: The teacher leads processing strategies and discussion to help students make sense of their work.
- Elaborate/Extend: Students extend or apply learning to new and real-world situations.
- Evaluate: Teacher brings closure, helping students summarize their work, make connections, and assess their learning.

Figure 2.1 provides an overview of how interactive notebooks support this approach to science instruction.

Figure 2.1   Interactive Notebooks and the 5E Learning Cycle

Day of Unit	Stage in 5E Learning Cycle	Instructional Activity	Corresponding Notebook Activity
1	Engage	Teacher introduces the science unit and discusses it briefly with the class.	Students complete a unit cover page as a homework assignment.
2	Engage	Teacher engages students in a trigger assignment to generate questions about the topic. The class develops a unit question or statement.	Students begin to construct the aha connections pages for the unit.
3	Engage, Explore, and Explain	Teacher provides key questions and students complete the first investigation. Teacher models how to write a summary statement, also known as an aha connections statement.	Students record their work related to this activity on the Input page. They record the aha connections statement for the investigation on one of the aha connections pages.
3	Elaborate/Extend	Teacher assigns homework based on the first investigation.	Students complete their homework on the first output page.
4–15	Engage, Explore, Explain, and Elaborate/Extend	Students complete additional lab activities in class, and teacher follows them up with homework assignments.	Students complete input and output pages for each activity. They also develop and record an aha connections statement for each activity.
16	Elaborate/Extend, and Evaluate	Teacher models for students how to write a self-reflection paper.	Students write a self-reflection paper.
17	Elaborate/Extend, and Evaluate	Teacher models for students how to write a thesis paper, also known as the aha thesis.	Students write an aha thesis.

MAKING CONNECTIONS FOR DEEPER UNDERSTANDING

Two key components of the interactive notebook are the "aha connections" pages and the "aha thesis." These terms may sound a little gimmicky, but I have found them to be effective with my students. These two components are the bookends of each unit in the interactive notebook—the aha connections pages are at the beginning of the unit and the aha thesis paper is at the end.

The aha connections pages reflect the central question for the unit as well as students' ongoing learning throughout the unit. To begin each unit, the teacher plans a trigger assignment, which is a high-interest activity intended to generate discussion and questions among the students. Following the trigger assignment, the teacher works with students to develop the essential question or problem the class has decided to answer during the unit. This question is written in the center of the aha connections pages. The unit then continues, and as students complete each lab activity, they write a summary and add it to the aha connections. Students also add other lines of evidence to the aha connections pages. However, students do more than simply write statements on these pages. They also show connections between concepts visually by using color, drawing arrows, and so on. Thus these pages become a place where students store their accumulated learning throughout the unit.

The aha connections pages become a rich resource students will use when they are ready to write the final, formal paper in the unit—the aha thesis. Chapter 7 explains more about the aha thesis assignment.

THE GENESIS OF THE "AHA" EXPERIENCE

My colleagues and I have noticed that students can write solid summaries and conclusions and even show evidence of making connections from one lab to the next, but often the processing is very linear. Students need assignments that take them beyond regurgitating factual information and increase their ability to make deeper connections and develop a better understanding of essential ideas—the big picture, so to speak. During a professional-development workshop, as my colleagues and I considered how to bridge the gaps for our students, we discussed a *Time Magazine* article titled, "How to Bring Our Schools Out of the 20th Century" (Wallis, 2006). The author addressed the need to help students:

- Know more about the world;
- Think outside the box;
- Become aware of new sources of information;
- Develop good people skills; and
- Develop new kinds of literacy skills.

The desire to incorporate these 21st-century skills and deepen student understanding led to the development of the aha connections and the aha thesis.

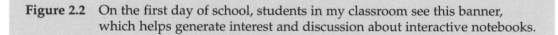

Figure 2.2   On the first day of school, students in my classroom see this banner, which helps generate interest and discussion about interactive notebooks.

THE AHA CONNECTIONS

Traditional science lessons often build on each other with one lesson leading to the next in a very linear fashion. In the real world, when you want to learn something, you gather information from multiple sources. For example, if you are in the market for a car, you might talk to your friends about how well they like their cars, you might review *Kelley Blue Book* prices and *Consumer Reports,* and you might test-drive several cars. Finally, you might go to several dealers to get the best pricing before you actually buy the car. Classroom learning should be no different. Students should be given the opportunity to gather information from multiple sources in order to come to a conclusion about a specific question or idea. Using the aha connections pages, students gather information from multiple sources, continually making connections until enough evidence has been collected to answer the central question or problem and write an aha thesis paper. The goal is to allow students to gather information from numerous sources in order to critically answer scientific problems.

Figure 2.3 shows the handout about the aha connections process. (See Reproducible 2 in Resource A for the actual handout.) The unit starts with a trigger that leads to the central question or problem for the unit. The graphic organizer on the handout shows an integrated compilation of evidence, which is nonlinear and includes examples of the types of evidence that students might use in order to answer the question. Evidence could be gathered from investigations, research, visuals, experts, and other sources. All of these lines of evidence will eventually lead to the aha thesis.

Figure 2.3   The Aha Connections Visual Outline

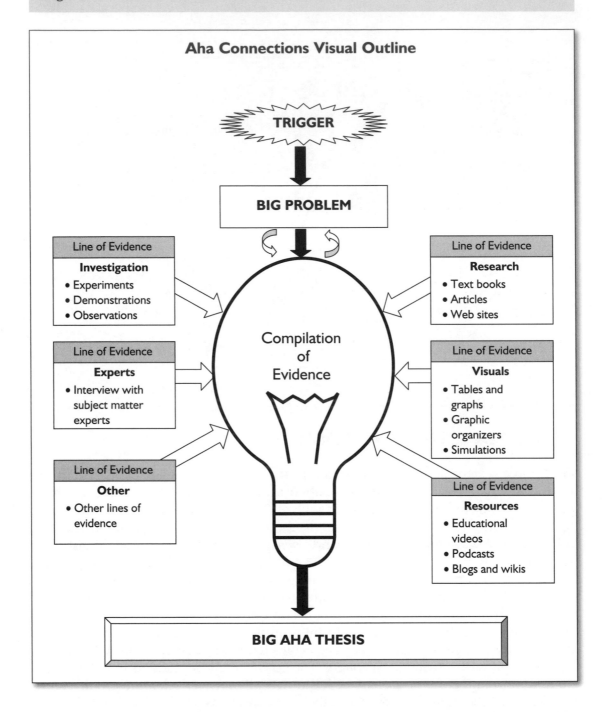

THE STEPS FROM THE
AHA CONNECTIONS TO THE AHA THESIS

Step 1: The Trigger

This is something that grabs the students' attention, sparking their interest and leading them to their question or big problem. In order to allow students an opportunity to find this spark, students need to be given time to do observations. The trigger that you use can be generated by visual observations, asking questions, reading, watching an educational video, interviews with a scientist, and so on. This provides an opportunity for buy in for all students. The goal is to develop a problem question that students will investigate in search of an answer.

Step 2: The Problem

The problem should include real-world issues. Problems don't necessarily need to result in one right answer, but the students should be able to gather evidence to support their answer. After students have an opportunity to look over their readings or visual observations, they start generating questions. These questions are summarized into one overarching question that students can now investigate. In a solid curriculum, this might be a unit concept in the form of a question. Some students will generate more than one question. Try to get the class to come to consensus on one question, but encourage the students to write their individual questions on sticky notes and hold on to those as well. Along with the main class questions, most individual questions will be answered during the investigations, which is exciting for some students.

Step 3: Gather Evidence to Back Up a Claim

Students can gather evidence from a variety of sources (as shown in the boxes on Figure 2.3). Traditionally, students get their primary evidence from lab experiments. There are, however, other sources that can be used to provide evidence and support or refute claims. Lines of evidence include (but are not limited to)

- Investigations (experiments, labs, and demonstrations);
- Research (from a textbook, other books, encyclopedias, Web sites, and magazines);
- Experts (interviews, phone, video, or e-mail conferences with scientists or researchers);
- Visuals (tables, graphic organizers, and simulators);
- Resources (educational videos, pod-casts, and blogs); and
- Others (any other source where students can find information).

Step 4: Compiling Evidence

Students gather all lines of evidence and find connections or conflicts among pieces of information. As students are compiling this information, they may find there are holes in their evidence and they need to do more research. Figure 2.4 shows the handout about constructing the aha connections pages. (See Reproducible 6 in Resource A for the actual handout.) Figure 2.5 shows an example of a student's aha connections pages.

Figure 2.4   Constructing the Aha Connections Pages. This handout, which students tape into the front of their notebook, shows what the aha connections pages should look like. I walk students through the aha connections concept and show examples of past aha connections pages.

Constructing the Aha Connections Pages

The Aha Connections pages are located at the beginning of each new unit in your Interactive Notebook.

First   Two side-by-side pages

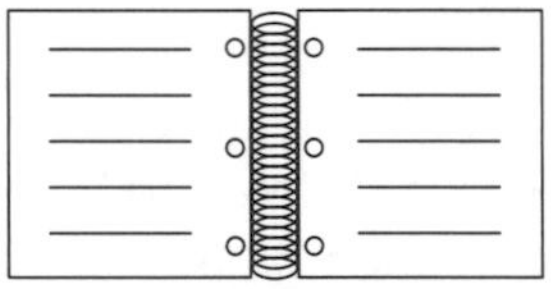

Second   In the center, or close to it, write your problem statement or big idea.

e.g., "What is an interaction?"

Third   After each class activity, you will be asked to write a statement that conveys the concept learned.

For example: "Today we learned that you can never obtain an exact value, but you can get very close. Scientists call this 'best value.'"

Fourth
- Take time to share out with a partner!
- Notice trends or connections!
- Use arrows or color to show those trends or connections visually! "Did this lab connect to the Big Aha problem, to another lab, or both?"

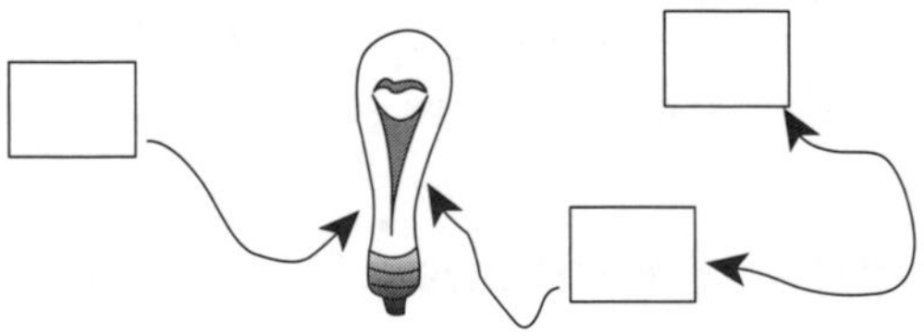

Last   Use these statements as evidence and stems to later write your aha thesis.

Step 5: The Aha Thesis

This assignment gives students an opportunity to be experts in the unit of study. Students can write their thesis as individuals or in teams. They take all of the lines of evidence that they have collected and compile them into a formal writing piece. The end result is a multiparagraph essay with an introductory paragraph, body paragraphs that summarize each line of evidence, and a closing paragraph. Students can use the lines of evidence as stems for writing their aha thesis. Information about how to write an aha thesis is found in Chapter 7. Reproducible A.6 is the handout students use as a guide when writing their aha thesis.

THE TRIGGER ASSIGNMENT

Each science unit starts with a trigger assignment, which can be implemented in a variety of ways. This might include watching a video, observing interactions (such as in an ant farm) and talking about what is happening, or giving a teacher demonstration of an interesting phenomenon. The goal is to build excitement in your students. The trigger will depend on what you are teaching and the grade level you teach. The science curriculum you use is one potential source of ideas for the trigger activity.

After the activity, you will facilitate a class discussion about what students just experienced. You will already have a preconceived idea about what the question or the "Big Aha" will be, so you will want to ask students preplanned questions in order to bring them to the same conclusion about what the problem will be for the unit. Make sure that you welcome all ideas that students mention. You might want to list the ideas on a chart so they are visible throughout the unit, and check them off as you discover evidence that supports or refutes the questions. This will demonstrate how the inquiry process in your science classroom is relevant to questions students generate about the world around them. When the class comes to consensus about the problem question, have students use the handout as a guide to begin to construct the aha connections pages.

Sometimes, my students have created a trigger page where they wrote ideas and questions they had about the upcoming unit so as to pique their interest and to begin to think about what the big question will be for the unit. What's nice about the trigger page is that anytime during the unit, students can go back and add their questions to the page. At the end of the unit, they can then reflect on how many questions were answered. Figure 2.6 shows a trigger question page.

Rather than reinventing the wheel to develop a trigger question, review the unit concepts in the existing science curriculum. Work with the students to help them rephrase one key concept into a researchable question, and then provide students with numerous opportunities to gather information from the various lines of evidence and formulate an answer to the question. These opportunities to develop nonlinear, global connections will help students develop a deeper understanding of the problem and its solutions.

After students write the central unit question or problem on their aha connections pages, the unit continues with lab explorations or activities. Chapter 4 will look

Figure 2.5   This figure shows a student example of two side-by-side aha connections pages. The problem is written in the middle, statements from each lab or line of evidence are shown around the problem, and arrows show connections between the ideas and the concepts learned throughout the unit. The student has used flip pages to include everything she wanted to say.

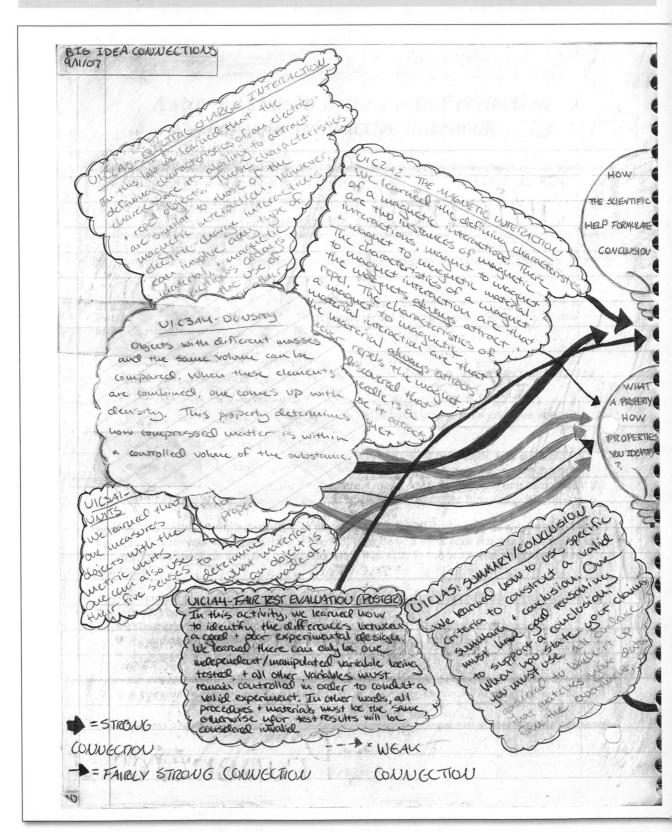

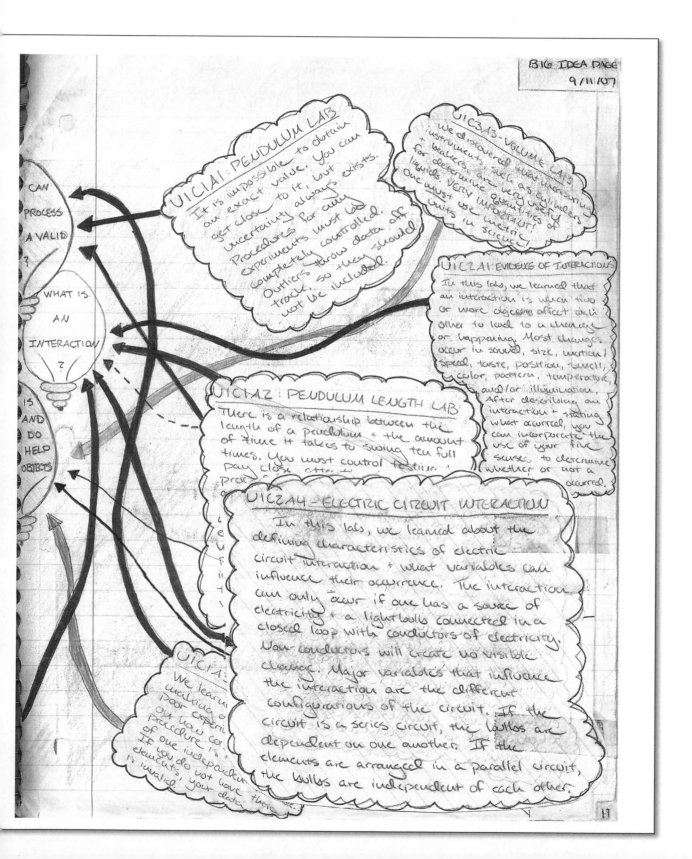

BIG IDEA PAGE
9/11/07

U1C1A1: PENDULUM LAB
It is impossible to obtain an exact value. You can get close to it, but uncertainty always exists. Procedures for any experiments must be completely controlled. Outliers throw data off track, so they should not be included.

U1C3A3 - VOLUME LAB
We discovered that measuring instruments such as cylinders + beakers are very useful for determining quantities of liquids. VERY IMPORTANT! One must use metric units in science!

U1C2A1: EVIDENCE OF INTERACTIONS
In this lab, we learned that an interaction is when two or more objects affect each other to lead to a change or happening. Most changes occur in sound, size, motion, speed, taste, position, smell, color, pattern, temperature and/or illumination. After describing an interaction + stating what occurred, you can incorporate the use of your five senses to determine whether or not a _____ occurred.

U1C1A2: PENDULUM LENGTH LAB
There is a relationship between the length of a pendulum + the amount of time it takes to swing ten full times. You must control testing. Pay close atten...

U1C2A4 - ELECTRIC CIRCUIT INTERACTION
In this lab, we learned about the defining characteristics of electric circuit interaction + what variables can influence their occurrence. The interaction can only occur if one has a source of electricity + a lightbulb connected in a closed loop with conductors of electricity. Non-conductors will create no visible change. Major variables that influence the interaction are the different configurations of the circuit. If the circuit is a series circuit, the bulbs are dependent on one another. If the elements are arranged in a parallel circuit, the bulbs are independent of each other.

U1C1A...
We learn... working ... Poor experi... out how co... Procedure is... of one independent... If you do not have... elements, your data... is invalid.

CAN I PROCESS A VALID ?

WHAT IS AN INTERACTION ?

IS AND DO HELP OBJECTS

11

Figure 2.6 This student kept a page full of questions on sticky notes. Every time he had a question, he wrote it down and stuck it on this page. Students who do this may return to the page to see if the questions were answered by the end of the unit.

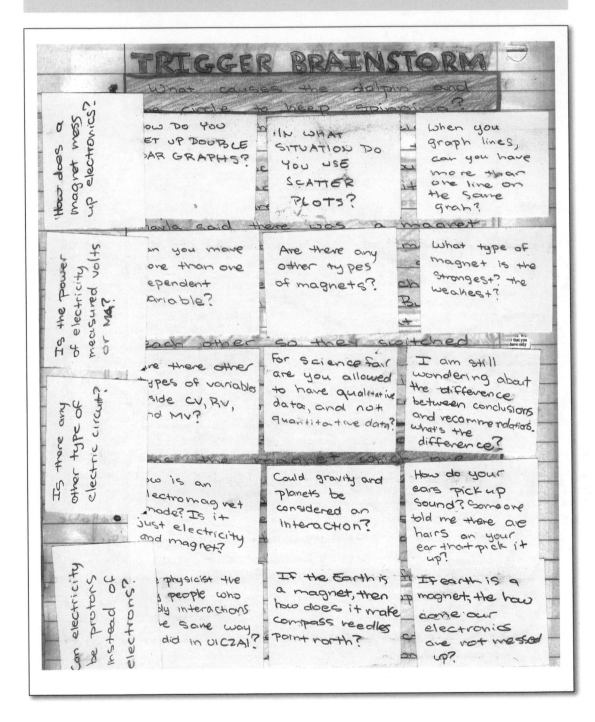

more closely at how to use the interactive notebook during lab activities. However, at this stage we want to consider how the lab activities relate to the aha connections. Each lab activity begins with a key question that targets the learning objective for the day. At the close of the lab activity, the teacher asks the students to write a statement that summarizes what they have learned. Here is one example of a class summary:

> We learned in this lab that there is a relationship between the length of a pendulum (IV) and the amount of time it takes to make 10 back-and-forth swings (DV). We also learned to pay close attention to the procedure and to control the testing to obtain an accurate "true value." We understand how scientists use uncertainty, average, and range in order to present the results to a given question or problem. Hypothesizing is a good idea before engaging in testing. The class learned how to graph our results correctly by following a given set of criteria, which includes a "this graph shows" and the use of independent and dependent variables.

Of course, some students will be more thorough than others, but the goal is for all students to document what they learned, so they can make connections to the central unit question or problem.

Students are asked to write each summary on their aha connections pages and use colors, arrows, picture icons, shapes, and so on to show connections from one idea to another idea or even to multiple ideas. The pages will begin to look like a graphic organizer. Students will not remember to complete this step on their own. This does not seem to work as a homework assignment, so you will need to provide five to ten minutes at the end of each class day for students to complete the exercise. Provide time as soon as the investigations are over, so the results are fresh in students' minds. One strategy is to have students write the statements on sticky notes, so the students can move them around as they make their connections or when they are organizing their work prior to writing the thesis. Another method is to ask the students to create a gigantic graphic organizer as a team.

One effective strategy is to create the aha connections graphic organizer (Figure 2.7) on a bulletin board, adding pieces after students complete each activity. You can model the writing the first time you do an aha connection by writing each statement after the activity with the class, posting it in the back of the room, asking the students where the connections go, and drawing in arrows accordingly.

USING THE TEACHER NOTEBOOK TO PLAN

Now that we have discussed the basic components of the science unit in the interactive notebook, we can consider strategies for planning lessons. As mentioned previously, most of the pages in the science unit are devoted to lab activities. However, these pages are preceded by the aha connections pages, where students will record the concepts they are learning during the unit and the connections between those concepts. The lab pages are followed by the self-reflection paper and the final formal writing assignment—the aha thesis.

Figure 2.7 This is an example of an aha page that was created with input from all the students in the classroom to help them learn how to write and connect concepts. This is a modeled activity and is intended to show students a concrete example of what making connections from activity to activity might look like in their notebooks.

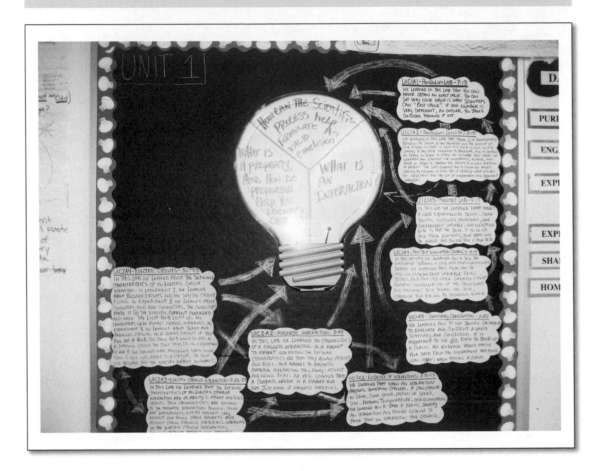

As you begin your unit planning, you will want to start with a solid idea of what the essential question (or the Big Aha) will be for the unit. This is the question you will be guiding your students toward at the beginning of the unit as the class decides what question or problem will be investigated. It is the question students will write in the center of their aha connections spread. For example, "What is an interaction?" Once you have determined the big question for the unit, you are ready to begin planning.

Plans for ongoing science instruction are developed and recorded in a teacher notebook. The teacher notebook provides a place to record all the activities students will do using their own interactive notebooks, as well as notes to yourself about questions that you plan to ask, hints for the lesson, or anything else you want to remember.

With the 5E Learning Cycle as the underlying structure, I use a backward design model as shown in Figure 2.8. I work through the steps from Step 1 through Step 9, thinking about the answers to the questions for each step.

Figure 2.8 Backward Design Using the 5E Learning Cycle

Lesson Concept or Focus Question	
Teacher Does	**Student Does**
(6) Engage: Develop questions or activities for kids that will produce a student goal for what you want them to do in the Engage step.	(2) Engage: How do you engage prior knowledge? What will the students do to connect to a prior lesson?
(7) Explore: Consider possible activities or prompts. How does this activity help students meet the goal?	(3) Explore: What are the students going to be doing? What do the kids need to explore? How will you take the students from where they are to where you want them to go?
(8) Explain: What are you going to ask or collect? What will let you know that the students understand?	(1) Explain: What will the students say, write, draw, do, . . . ?
(9) Elaborate/Extend: What could you do and/or have students do to show an understanding of a new situation?	(4) Elaborate/Extend: Apply the knowledge learned to a new situation.

Question: Does Step 6 get you to Step 3? What kinds of work are you generating?

(5) Decision-Point Assessment (DPA):
If the students don't give you what you want to hear, what are you going to do?

Start your planning by asking, "What do I want the students to say about what they learned as they leave the room? What do I want them to know? What will this sound like in student language? What key scientific language will I want to hear?" The answers to these questions become the lesson concept.

Next, think about what the students will say, draw, and write at the end of the lesson. This becomes the Explain for what the student does in the backwards-design lesson planning, or Step 1. Whatever work the students are generating, these are the things you would like to hear them saying at the end of the day.

After identifying these ideas, move to the Engage portion of the lesson, keeping in mind what you want from the students. (Do not think about what *you* will do yet; think about what the *student does*.) For Step 2, ask yourself, "What will the students do to connect to a prior lesson?" This phase of the lesson usually begins with a key question.

In Step 3, move to the Explore phase where you ask yourself, "What are the students going to be doing that will take them from where they are to where I want them to go?" This student work will be reflected on the input page of the notebook. Think about what it will look like, and sketch a template in your teacher notebook. (Use pencil). As you teach the lesson, you can make changes to the page format. You can add to or change specific aspects of the page to better fit what the students need in that particular lesson.

Step 4 is the Elaborate or Extend portion of the lesson. Think about what you want the students to do to apply their new knowledge learned to a new situation. This is usually the work students will complete on the output page of the student notebook, and oftentimes, this is homework. This is the phase during which I think about the metacognitive aspect of each lesson.

At Step 5, begin to think about decision-point assessment. If the students do not give you what you want to hear, what are you going to do? What questions will you ask, what alternate direction will you take, and so on?

After thinking about the students and what they will do in Steps 1 through 5, think about what you will do as the teacher.

Steps 6 through 9 are about what the teacher does in the Engage phase. What questions do you plan to ask, what activities will you provide, and what is the set up for the lesson?

Step 7 asks what possible activities or prompts you will lead the students through. And more importantly, how do these activities help your students meet the lesson goal?

For Step 8, ask yourself what work will students complete that will let you know whether they understand the key concepts.

Last, in Step 9, what could you ask your students to do that would show an understanding of how the concept relates to a new situation? After working your way through this process and designing the notebook pages (using the existing curriculum), three final steps will help ensure an effective lesson:

1. Write questions you will ask the students during the circulation phase of the lesson.

2. Brainstorm expected student responses. Do the questions you wrote push students to higher levels of thinking?

3. Identify where, during the lesson, you have provided opportunities for student-to-student interaction.

Thinking about these questions will help you design each notebook page. I usually plan for students' engage and explore work to be presented on the input (right-side) notebook pages. Sometimes, I put explain work on the right side too—it depends on the lesson. I always have students complete the elaborate and extend work on the output (left side) of the notebook because these correlate with the metacognitive elements of each lesson. Evaluate, the fifth E, should be ongoing and woven throughout each lesson and the entire notebooking process.

The teacher notebook serves several purposes. First, as stated above, it is a place for your lesson plans—complete, well-thought-out lesson plans that include reasons for asking students to do the work they do. Your plans will have a purpose, focus, and include the 5Es. Your teacher notebook is a tool of learning, similar to the student notebooks. At the end of the year, all of your lessons will be in the same spot. You can learn and grow from the lessons you used because the entirety of each lesson is there, including what the students did. Traditional lesson plans have spaces to write the date, the time, and the lesson focus, but very rarely do you have the opportunity to see the lesson in its entirety including notes you jot down as you teach and augment the lesson. In the following year, you can use your notebook from the previous year to build on the lessons and improve them. Each year you will be improving your own practice.

The teacher notebook is also useful when students miss class. Since the pages are numbered, dated, labeled, and have a template of what the students do on each given day, you can show the student who was absent your teacher notebook and they can probably (with the use of the curriculum and possibly some supplies) recreate the assignment in their own student interactive notebook. It won't be the same as if the student was present during the original activity, but the teacher notebook facilitates helping a student make up missed work. You may need to help the student answer questions, but the process is easier than starting from scratch.

One additional benefit of the teacher notebook—it will help you see the gaps in your lessons. Because each lesson is laid out in front of you, you can readily see the connections between the different lessons as well as between the different units. You can verify that each lesson builds on the next and moves the learning along. If the students are having difficulty making connections, you can easily see where you might need to add input. Identifying flaws is easier when you are able to review the entire lesson rather than just isolated concepts.

SUMMARY

Interactive notebooks are organized to increase learning by ensuring that students make connections between key concepts in science. The aha connections and the aha thesis help facilitate the process by which students develop deep understandings of the interrelatedness of important ideas. Teachers can plan the use of interactive notebooks using the 5E Learning Cycle as a framework. Plans are recorded in a teacher notebook, which mirrors the work students will do in their own notebooks. Key points to remember include

- Use the 5E Learning Cycle as the framework for lessons.
- Develop science units around the aha connections.
- Help students identify a problem to solve that connects to real-world issues.
- Plan for students to gather evidence from a variety of sources and continually make connections.
- Give students an opportunity to synthesize their thinking in a way that addresses the big problem for the unit.
- Build the skills students will need in the 21st century.

3

Gaining Student Buy In and Ownership

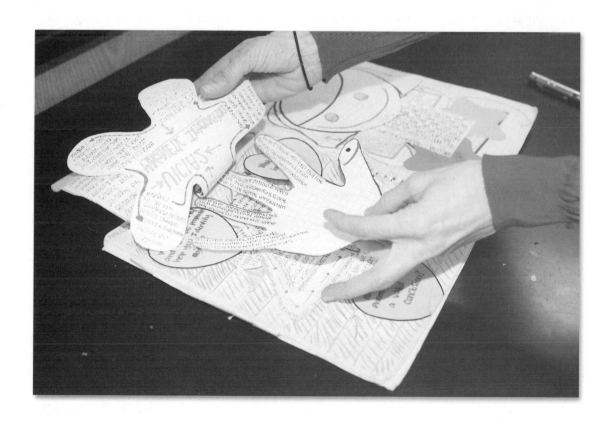

A key ingredient for successful notebooking is gaining student buy in and own-ership. Student ownership provides the opportunity for teachers to expect more effort from their students. Without this, many students will make a minimal effort, looking for the easiest and fastest way to whatever letter grade they are accustomed to earning. In my experience, human nature dictates giving the minimum output necessary to receive the maximum results. However, minimal effort typically means minimal growth and correlates with a lack of opportunity for students to stretch their minds and achieve at their highest potential.

Student pride and ownership is built from the start of the notebooking process. For students to own the process, the notebooks must be personal. Every page, while meeting the expectations established by the teacher, should also be personalized by the student. This personalization can be achieved in many ways, as I will explain in this chapter.

PERSONALIZING THE INTERACTIVE NOTEBOOK VISUAL PAGE

One early opportunity for students to personalize their notebooks is the comple-tion of the interactive notebook visual page, which is taped in the front of their notebooks. Students will complete this page as a homework assignment during the first week of class. (More information about the process for introducing note-books to students and completing this page may be found in Chapter 6.) This page shows the thinking processes students will be using when working in their interactive notebooks. In the center of the page is a picture of a student thinking. The most personal thing that I can think of is a photo, so I ask each student to affix his or her picture in the middle of the page over the picture of the student on the handout. This helps reinforce the idea that each student is responsible for the work in his or her notebook. The student's photo on one of the first pages of the interactive notebook is there for all to see. Students get excited about this and love coming to school the next day and showing everyone the picture they chose to represent themselves. Figure 3.1 shows an example of a student's photo.

PERSONALIZING UNIT COVER PAGES

Another opportunity to personalize notebooks and promote ownership is the cre-ation of unit cover pages. Students make a new cover page at the beginning of each unit. The cover page includes the unit title. For example, the first unit of the year might be titled "Measurement and Data Collection." Students put that title on the cover page and must also include one or more graphics that relate to the title. Hand-drawn graphics are preferred, but students think it's cool to use computer-generated graphics, which are also acceptable. The illustrations need to be appropriate for the title of the unit. For the unit on measurement and data collection, students could draw measuring tools used in science, such as rulers, beakers, cylinders, scales, and so on. They could also draw a graph or a data table because these relate to the title. However, pictures of Mickey Mouse or SpongeBob SquarePants are out of the

Figure 3.1 Whether students use sports photos, photos of themselves making silly faces, or pictures from a trip, the photograph makes the notebook more personal. Some students put frames around their pictures, which is a nice touch.

question. I tell students they must color the page from "corner to corner." This means that the entire page is colored, with no white from the notebook paper showing. The students may use colored pencils or a light crayon to shade the background of the page. (Markers are not permitted as they will bleed through and can be more difficult for students to work with.) I realize this might seem a bit obsessive, but I've found that requiring a completely colored page forces students to take their time thinking about the new ideas they will have the opportunity to explore in the upcoming unit. Additionally, corner-to-corner coverage makes the page more attractive and increases the likelihood that students will take pride in the artwork they've completed. Kids love to draw and color, and giving them the opportunity to do this in their science notebooks benefits them by promoting ownership. Furthermore, students are completely free to choose how to represent the unit on the cover page. Only the title is chosen by the teacher; the rest is up to the students, making the cover pages extremely personal.

Figure 3.2   This image and the next show examples of cover pages generated by students. This student preferred drawing her cover page.

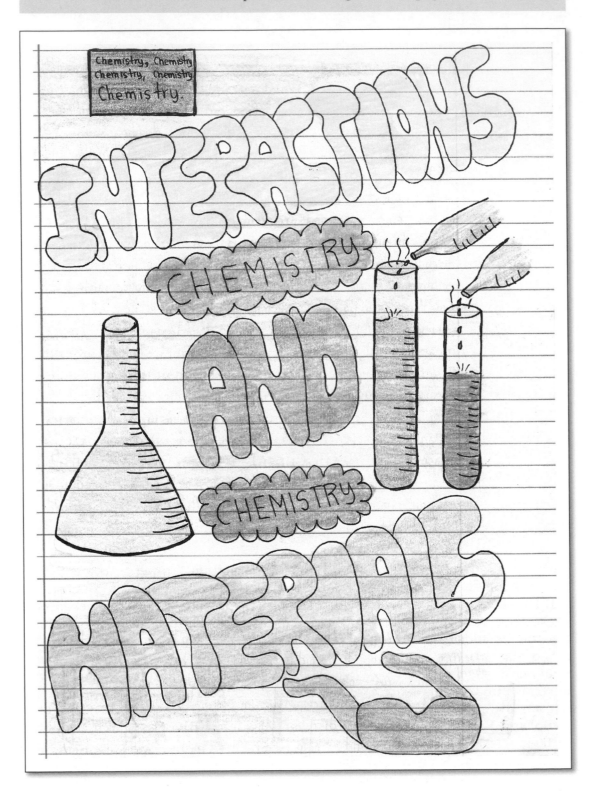

Figure 3.3   This student enjoyed finding pictures to tape onto his cover page. Students' cover pages are usually very different and quite unique to the individual student.

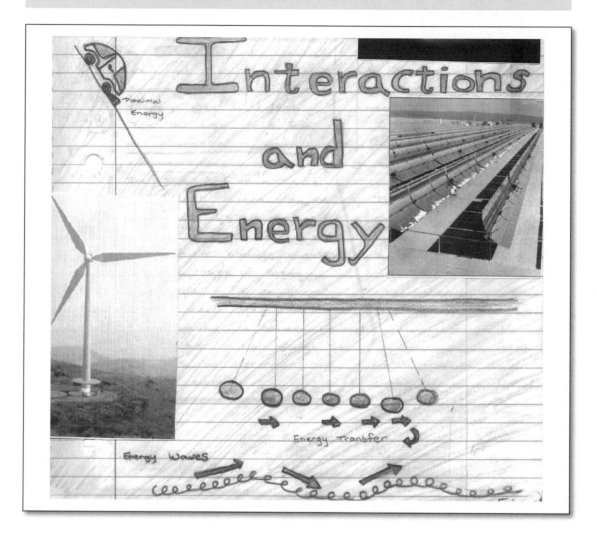

Celebrating student work is important. For example, marching a student to another class to show off his or her cover page can be fun. Most students love the attention that their work generates. This is all part of the student buy-in process. If you work hard at this during in the first few weeks of school, it will pay off later in the year when students are giving you their all.

VALUING IDEAS AND PROMOTING COMMUNITY

Another way to create ownership is to value students' ideas. Celebrate work done well either individually or as a group. You can celebrate with simple statements, such as, "Hey kids, when you get a chance, take a look at page 71 in Tori's notebook; she really took our ideas to a new level," or "Team B is on to something that no other group has thought about yet. Why don't we give the team members a moment to share and let us in on their thinking?" You can take this kind of recognition a step further by asking individual students to share specific pages with the class. Or, after teaching a new concept, have the students who really understand the concept share their knowledge with their classmates. This student-to-student interaction is a powerful motivator for the students doing the sharing, and it can be a helpful learning tool for the other students. Peer teaching is particularly helpful if the concept is one you realize you may need to reteach. I like to take advantage of the fact that many students love the opportunity to teach. Just remember to try to give all students an opportunity for this during the year rather than choosing the same students repeatedly.

Figure 3.4   During one investigation, we used electrolysis to separate the oxygen from the hydrogen in water by collecting and testing the gases produced from a flame interaction. This student made a note to find other possible compounds to break down and test. She wanted to present the findings in front of the class by making connections to prior explorations. How cool is that! She wanted to be the teacher!

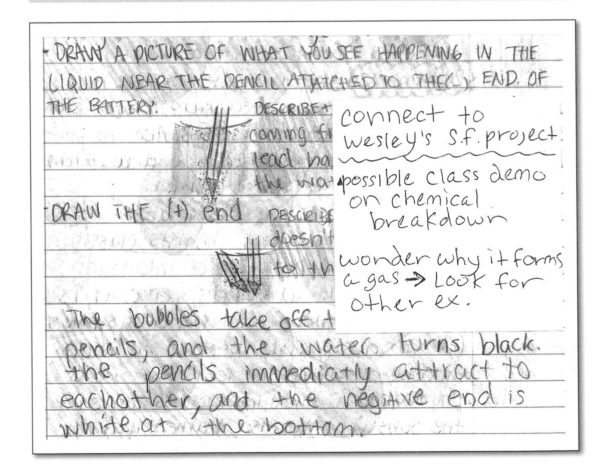

Teamwork also helps with student buy in, especially at the beginning of the school year, because it allows students to feel safe. Students exchange ideas with each other and collaborate on ways to represent the work they are doing. They support one another and continue to build confidence throughout the year. Students don't want to let a teammate down, so they try harder to maintain focus for the success of the group, which in turn produces better notebooks and better evidence of student learning.

Allowing students to take an idea and run with it is another way to encourage ownership. Imagine, for example, a student comes to you and asks, "Can I use a classroom computer to create a movie about solids, liquids, and gases?" There are several possible ways to respond to this question. You may say, "Yes," and then allow the student to work independently and share his or her work with the class when it is completed. Or, you might say, "Hey class, Joel had an idea to make a movie about solids, liquids, and gases. Does anyone else have a similar idea? Why don't you work together as a group to come up with something that you could present to the class at the end of the week?" If time allows, and you were already planning to do something similar, you may say, "Hey class, Joel just came up with a great idea. He thought it would be cool to make a movie about solids, liquids, and gases. What do you think? Should we go for it?" You would then set up the criteria, establish a time frame, and let the learning begin.

These are powerful ways to celebrate student work and student ideas. When students generate their own ideas, and those ideas are recognized and encouraged, their learning will increase, and they will gain confidence and an awareness of their own intellectual capacity. Plus, being given the opportunity to explore, create, and present their own work encourages students to feel more like real scientists.

CHOICE, CONNECTIONS, AND CREATIVITY

Notebooks can be used to offer students choice, to encourage their creativity, and to help them make connections, all of which promote ownership. For example, students have multiple opportunities to choose how to represent their work in a variety of different ways. They may use pictures, color, highlighting, underlining, sticky notes, tabbing, and flip pages (which are discussed in Chapter 6).

In addition, the assignments encourage them to make connections to their own lives. For example, they might connect the concepts studied in class to something they do at home every day (e.g., practicing the piano or making afterschool snacks). Another way to encourage connections is to have students allocate a page for their own questions and ideas. This "free" page is a place for their own ideas, uncensored by you or anyone else.

It is important to remember that a student's notebook is not your personal work, and it may not look exactly as you think it should. You may not see what you expect to see. But, providing students with choices about how to do notebooking is essential. Over time, you will see evidence of in-depth work that includes student connections to prior work, complete sentences, extensions of ideas, and attempts at extra credit through at-home explorations or problem solving.

Figure 3.5 This student used color, shading and personalized bullets to make her lists.

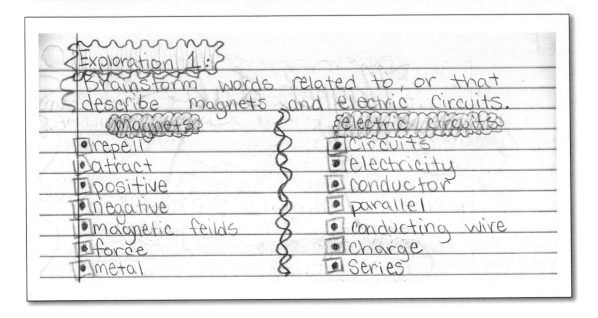

Figure 3.6 This student used outlines, arrows, and a graphic to describe an elastic interaction.

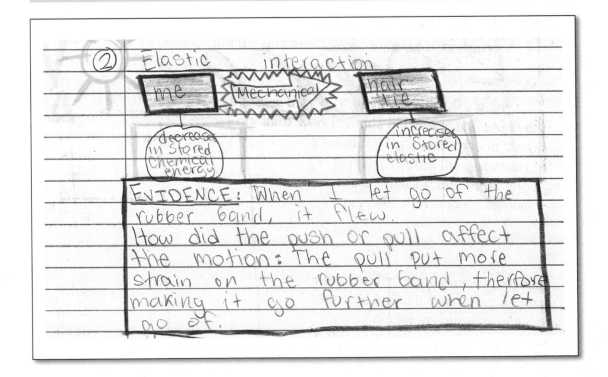

Figure 3.7 This student used a sticky note as a reminder of a prior lab that explored friction. This allowed her to make a connection and reference that connection later in a conversation or maybe in a written reflection.

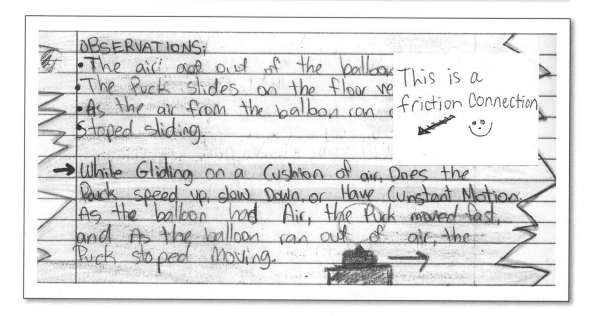

THE NEED FOR FLEXIBILITY

Teachers have a lot of material to cover in a short amount of time, and it's difficult to not feel the pressure to keep moving in order to address all of the standards, but it is the real-life experiences and connections that allow students to gain ownership of certain content. Although it takes time, if you allow a student to produce original ideas and work from those ideas, you can use that time as a teachable moment and find a way to connect that student's idea to a standard. If a student's idea came from your class, it most likely stemmed from one of the standards you were already addressing.

When you nurture and cultivate hard work and demonstrate your discipline, it is likely that classroom problems will be at an all-time low, which saves you even more time! So, be flexible and find a way to make these sidetracks of original thinking fit into the regular flow of your daily plans. You should see greater overall effort, students who are more motivated and on task in class, and an increase in sharing ideas and collaboration.

A BY-PRODUCT OF OWNERSHIP

One of the by-products of a high degree of notebook ownership is an increase in neatness and organization. As the year goes on, some students develop specific strategies and become more methodical in order to keep their notebook neat and organized. For example, a student may prefer to write in pencil and then, in the end, go over the work in pen and color. Students may also add any written work to their original existing ideas. It can become difficult to find self-corrections in student work at times because of the obsessions that the students acquire throughout the year. You may also notice many students coming to the classroom prepared and ready to work with all of their tools for success (e.g., colored pencils, scissors, tape, sticky notes). In addition, some students' notebooks will become neater as the year progresses. The notebooks students start in September are the ones they will still be carrying in May, which means some notebooks may require extensive bandaging by the end of the year. I have seen students carry their notebooks around in folders or even three ring binders to keep them from falling apart. It's exciting to see students working so hard to stay organized.

Pride comes from work well done; ownership comes from the opportunity to make it their own. If you celebrate their accomplishments and provide the opportunity, you will achieve student buy in. When you have student buy in, you have a chance to work with kids who care about the work they do. Students are at their best when they care about their work, which is all you can ask for.

Figure 3.8   This sample shows tabs and how some students mark the beginning of units or important pages throughout their notebooks.

Evidence of in-depth work includes student connections to prior work, complete sentences, extensions of ideas, and attempts at extra credit through at-home explorations or problem solving. Figure 3.9 shows how a student's work on a homework assignment generated a possible question for a science fair project.

Figure 3.9 When completing a homework assignment, this student was triggered to think about an upcoming science fair project. (The initials S.F.Q. stand for "Science Fair Question.") When she is working on her project for the next six months, it will be more meaningful because it is something she thought of on her own and was interesting to her. Without the notebook, the ideas may have been lost forever, thrown away like so many loose papers.

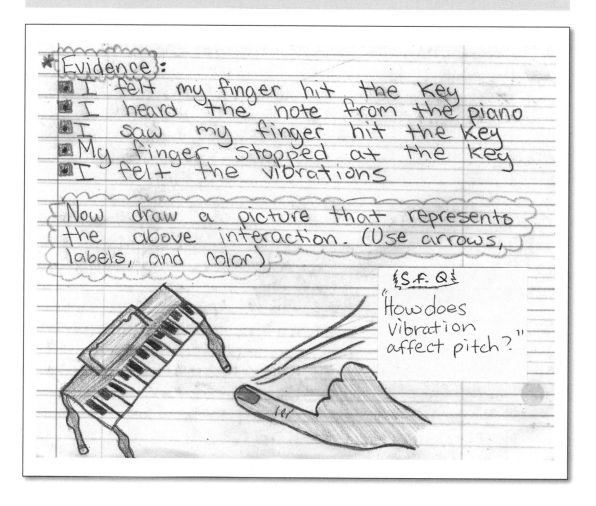

SUMMARY

Buy in and ownership are key to student success in using interactive notebooks, allowing the teacher to push students to work harder and think more rigorously. Start to encourage this ownership right away, from day one. When working toward gaining student buy in, remember to

- Make it personal; *personal* means that students' notebooks represent them and the work they do;
- Celebrate student work; when you see a notebook page that deserves praise because the level of the work exceeded expectations, be generous!

- Value students' unique ideas and provide opportunities for follow-through;
- Encourage connections to real-life experiences, and model what those might look and sound like;
- Be flexible, allowing students to drive the conceptual flow in your classroom occasionally; they will put more effort into their work, and you can bet it will be their best; and
- Use teams to build confidence and move timid students into the active waters of participation.

4

Using Notebooks During Investigations

I n Chapter 2, we looked at the first steps in a science unit: the trigger assignment and the initial construction of the aha connections pages. After these activities are completed, the science unit continues as students engage in lab investigations each day.

A CLASSROOM INVESTIGATION

To give you an idea of how interactive notebooks are used, I will describe a lab in which students explored the ideas behind an electric-charge interaction. Figure 4.1 shows the key question, which was, "What are some defining characteristics of the electric-charge interaction?"

Figure 4.1 The key question introduces the concept that will be the focus of the day and draws students into the lesson. Students write an answer to the question on their own, pair-share it, and then we discuss some of the ideas as a class. Students draw a key symbol next to the key question.

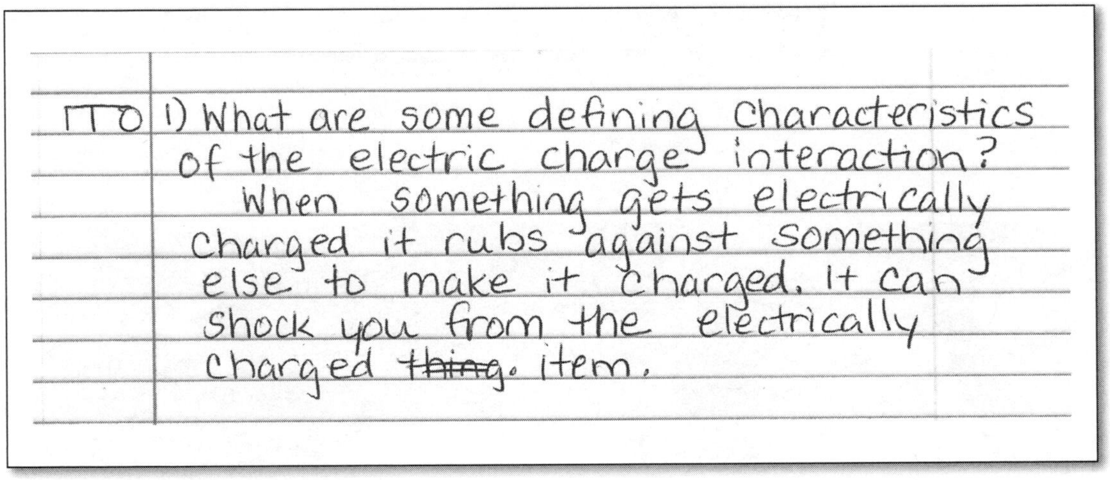

> 🔑 1) What are some defining characteristics of the electric charge interaction?
> When something gets electrically charged it rubs against something else to make it charged. It can shock you from the electrically charged ~~thing.~~ item.

The previous day, the students had explored magnetic interactions, so the second question asked in this lab, before the actual experimentation, was, "Based on what we discussed about electric-charge interactions, what do you think might be some of the similarities or differences between the magnetic and electric-charge interactions?" Both of these questions were asked during the engage part of the lesson.

The students went on to explore electric-charge interactions by charging a balloon with a small piece of wool and testing how different types of materials, both metallic and nonmetallic, interacted with the charged balloon. They recorded their observations of what happened in various ways (the students chose how they wanted to collect this information). Figures 4.2, 4.3, and 4.4 show how students recorded their observations.

Figure 4.2   This student chose to record his observations using a data table.

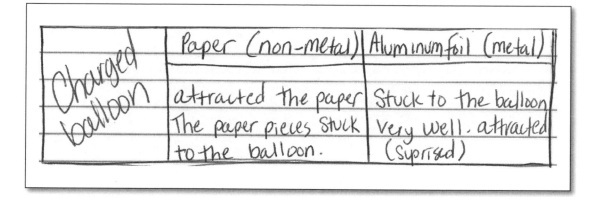

Charged balloon	Paper (non-metal)	Aluminum foil (metal)
	attracted the paper. The paper pieces stuck to the balloon.	Stuck to the balloon very well. attracted (suprised)

Figure 4.3   This student chose to bullet her observations.

- the charged balloon attracted the bits of paper.
- the charged balloon attracted the bits of aluminum.
- the non-charged balloon did nothing, the paper and aluminum were still.

After the students collected these observations, they responded to the following questions in their interactive notebook:

- What happens when a charged object (balloon) is brought near nonmetallic and metallic objects that are not charged?
- Do you think that electrically charged objects behave the same way as two magnets, or differently? Why do you think so?

The responses to the second question varied, but most students thought that they behave differently. One student said, "Magnets always have a magnetic force in them without something happening, and electrically charged things have to have something done to them to make them electrically charged." Another student replied, "Plus, electrically charged objects can attract but not repel."

Figure 4.4   This student chose to show his observations visually, with labels.

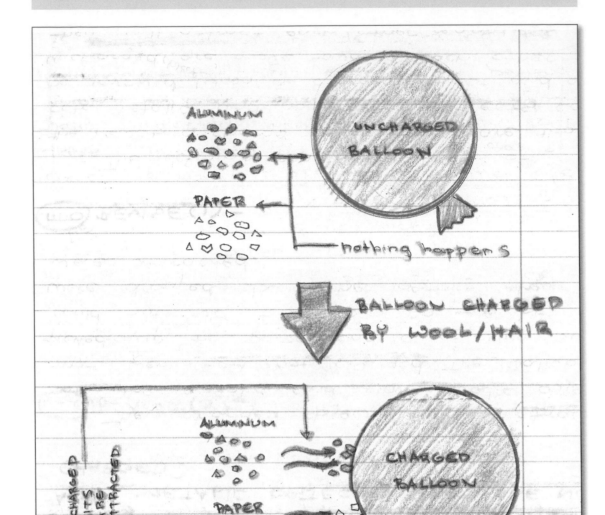

Because the students had not fully grasped the ideas, as evidenced by their responses, I moved to the next phase of the lab where students explored more electric-charge interactions by observing electrically charged tape. This was still part of the explore phase. Students were asked to collect data from the sticky and nonsticky sides of electrically charged tape in terms of their interactions to each other. As students collected data, I walked around from table to table asking probing questions to assess student understanding and more effectively guide students to their final ideas about electrically charged interactions. A few examples of these questions:

- "What can you tell me about why some pieces of tape repel and some attract?" This higher-level question generated a response that led to more questions and forced the students to think about what was happening.
- "How did the tape become charged?" This lower-level question is process oriented and forced the students to think about what was happening, how they got there, and perhaps about the procedure and variables if the test was not going as expected.
- "What are some characteristics of this type of interaction?" This middle-level question helped me redirect students and keep them focused on the main concept of the day.

Other possible questions for this exploration include

- Does the mass of the charged object influence the interaction in any way? If so, how?
- What happens when you flip the tape?
- What additional questions do you have as a result of your observations?
- What do you know for certain?
- What evidence do you have that supports that certainty?
- Can you explain what is happening that allows this interaction to occur?
- How does the distance between the two pieces of tape relate to the interaction?
- What are you uncertain about?
- Did these activities cause you to change your thinking about the similarities and differences between magnetic and electric-charge interactions?

The questions above could have been used to elicit written responses in the interactive notebooks or as probing questions asked by the teacher when circulating during the exploration.

After the investigation was complete, I revisited the key question from the opening and asked students to compose a written response in their interactive notebooks, giving evidence from the lab that supported their ideas. We ended the day with a whole-class consensus conversation about our findings, and I assigned homework requiring metacognitive processing for the output (left-side) page. I asked the students to write a conclusion, using specific criteria and their evidence, about electric-charge interactions. (I will go into detail about conclusion writing in Chapter 7, Learning Through Writing.)

DEVELOPING STUDENT THINKING

In this example, the exploration with the electrically charged balloons and tape is not about how to electrically charge objects but about the unique characteristics of an electric-charge interaction and how it is different from other types of interactions. We explored how magnetic interactions can be similar but can also be classified as different. I wanted students to see the bigger picture about how to categorize different interactions and distinguish differences between various types of interactions.

At the end of the exploration, the bottom line was whether the students could articulate the important concepts from the activity provided. Could they answer the key question I asked at the beginning of the lesson more accurately, using examples from the exploration?

One student's initial response to the question, "What are the defining characteristics of an electric-charge interaction?" was, "I think the defining characteristic of the electric-charge interaction is probably the special characteristics of it. For example, a magnet does not attract hair, but electric-charge interaction does." His revised answer at the end of the investigation is shown in Figure 4.5.

Figure 4.5 This student is now able to give specifics from the lab that identify the characteristics of an electric-charge interaction. He goes into detail about "like" charges and what that will cause in terms of an interaction with electrically charged objects.

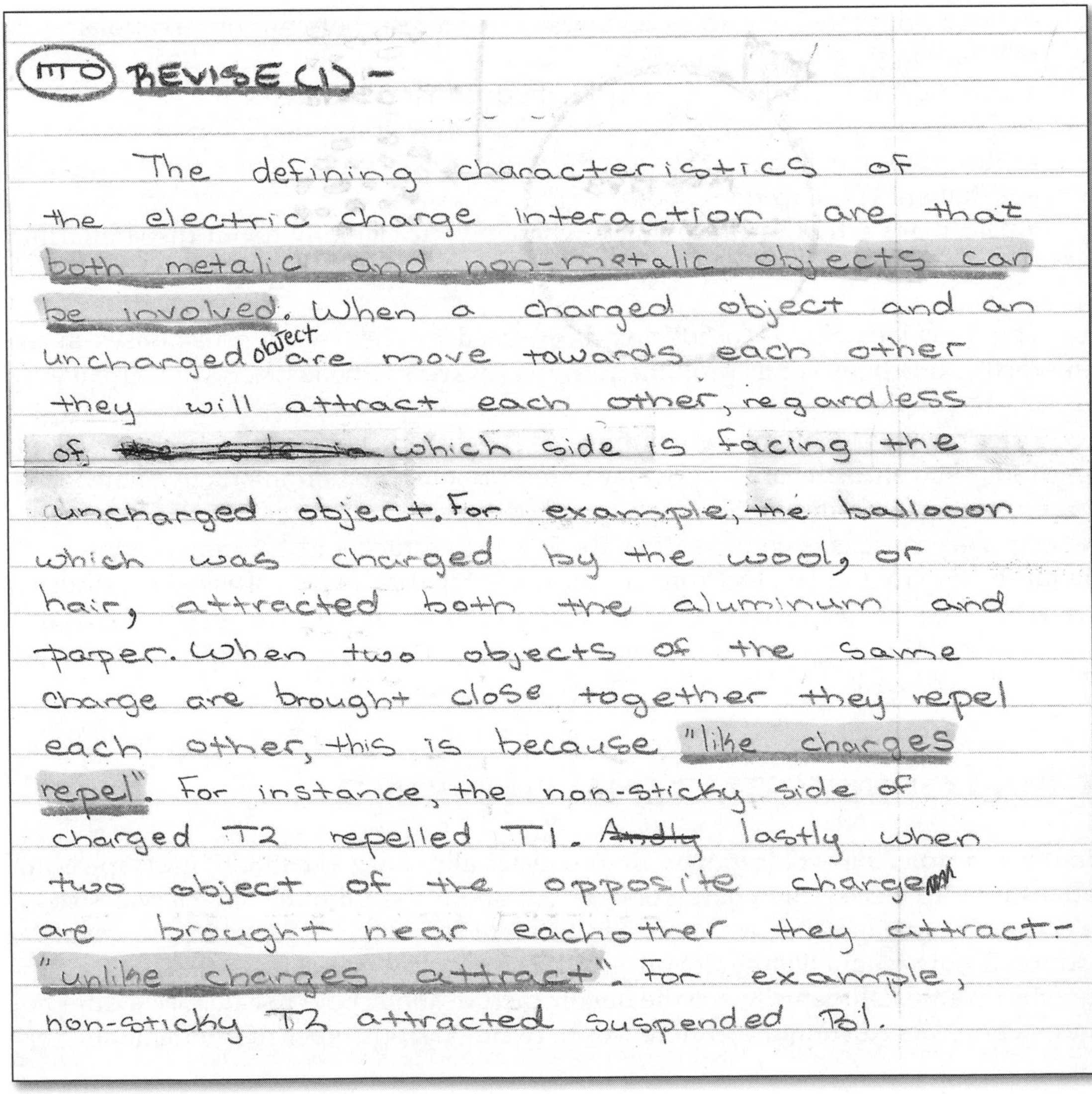
ITO REVISE (1) -

The defining characteristics of the electric charge interaction are that both metalic and non-metalic objects can be involved. When a charged object and an uncharged object are move towards each other they will attract each other, regardless of ~~the side in~~ which side is facing the uncharged object. For example, the ballooon which was charged by the wool, or hair, attracted both the aluminum and paper. When two objects of the same charge are brought close together they repel each other, this is because "like charges repel". For instance, the non-sticky side of charged T2 repelled T1. ~~Andly~~ lastly when two object of the opposite charges are brought near eachother they attract: "unlike charges attract". For example, non-sticky T2 attracted suspended B1.

The second question during the engage portion of this lesson was, "What are some of the similarities and differences between a magnetic and electric-charge interaction?" This student initially replied, "They are similar because they both attract objects. They are similar because they both do not repel nonmagnetic material. They are different because a magnet cannot attract hair." Figure 4.6 shows the revised answer completed by the student at the end of the investigation. He is now able to provide a detailed explanation of the similarities and differences between the two types of interactions.

Figure 4.6 The student is able to go into detail explaining both the similarities and differences between the two types of interactions. He recalls information from a prior lab where we tested different materials on magnets and uses that information to further explain his ideas.

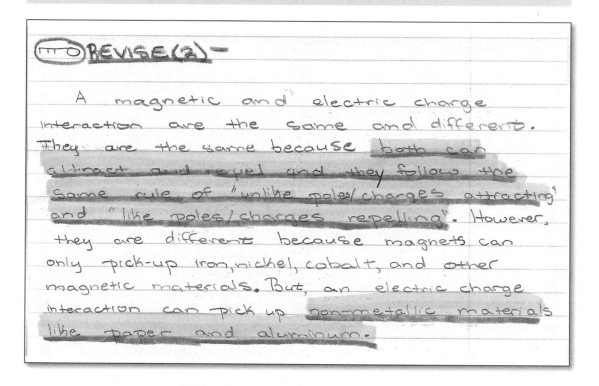

ENGAGE AND EXPLORE: A CLOSER LOOK AT THE INPUT PAGE

In Figure 2.1, we saw how work in interactive science notebooks correlates with the 5E Learning Cycle. Student work related to the engage and explore phases is displayed on right-side notebook pages. Sometimes, I ask students to explain work on the right side too—it depends on the lesson. Another way to think of this is that the right side of the notebook is the "teacher input" or "facilitated learning" side. It seems natural to show the teacher facilitated work (input) on the right side of the notebook and the metacognitive work (output) on the left because people typically begin writing on the right side, or front, of a page rather than the back.

The input pages on the right side show all the work we might expect to see in a traditional science notebook: the teacher-guided work students do to begin exploring and thinking. Naturally, some elements of experimental design and guided or scaffolded questions are reflected in the work on this side of the interactive notebook. For example, students include the hypotheses, procedures, variables, observations, and data collection on this side. Students will then be expected to process the day's work and use the information to formulate their conclusions and opinions on the left side.

Figure 4.7 The right-side page of the notebook shows student observations about magnetism and static electricity. The left-side page shows the student's understanding (making meaning) of the relationships between magnetic and electric charge interactions.

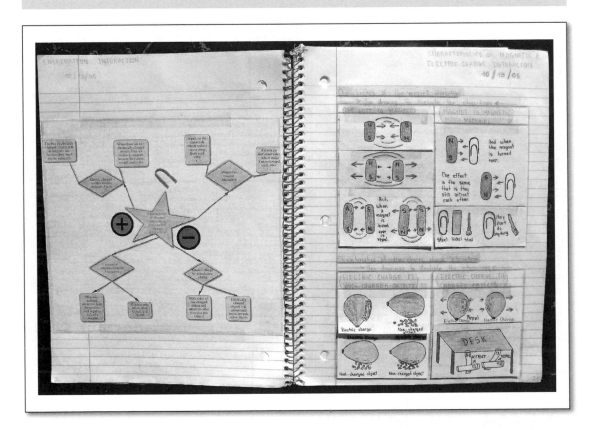

The work students do on the input pages should reflect their engagement in an inquiry lesson that leads to self-discovery. Developing the template for accomplishing this can be challenging. To reach this goal, you will want to keep these things in mind:

- All notebook pages should align with the standards. Also, all pages should reflect a conceptual flow of the material being taught throughout the year.
- Use the curriculum you have available to plan the student work and develop the page. Although you may need to augment the curriculum, there is no need

to reinvent the wheel when it comes to the basic elements of experimental design.

- The right side of students' notebooks may also vary depending on the lesson focus. You may not always find all elements of experimental design included in every lesson; you can choose which elements to focus on.

For example, if you were teaching a lesson on compounds, and the objective was for students to describe the properties of compounds, and then (on the left-side page) identify the differences between an element and a compound, you might want the written work on the right side to take the form of observations or procedures. In this particular lab, a hypothesis, or the identification of the independent and dependent variable, may not be important.

THE ROLE OF QUESTIONS

Questioning is the heart of the input phase of the lesson. Good questions are essential to probing students for understanding, which you want reflected on the right side of the interactive notebook. You will want to incorporate different kinds of questions—both lower-level and higher-level questions—throughout the lesson. Lower-level questions may ask students to identify or list aspects of the targeted concept, whereas the higher-level questions focus students on finding relationships or classifying ideas. The highest level of questioning should be present on the left side of the notebook where you target students' metacognition and ask them to expand on their ideas or create something new that originates from the thinking shown on the right-side page.

You can integrate all types of questions throughout the lesson; but for the input pages, try to design questions that elicit more than a one-word response or only one right answer. The best questions engage students in both giving an answer and using evidence to explain their thinking.

I might start by asking students to think about how they would go about solving a given problem. Next, I might ask them to compare or contrast the ideas of today's lesson to previous labs, or even inquire about what caused a particular interaction to occur. Then, I might conclude the lab with a question such as, "If you were to continue this test, or change the variable, what do you think the results might be? Why?" Finally, I might ask students to cite similar examples they have noticed in the world and to describe how the real-world examples relate to the lab example.

During planning, you should also script questions you might ask to probe for student understanding as you circulate throughout the classroom during the investigation. These questions do not need to be answered in the interactive notebook. Instead, they will usually take the form of clarifying questions, such as asking students what they mean by the terms they are using, asking them to walk you through their thinking, or to explain how they reached a particular conclusion. I have found that as I plan more, my questioning skills have improved, and I have been able to provide more meaningful opportunities to help my students increase their understanding.

Planning for student responses allows you to formulate a few questions to follow up or redirect those students who stray, have difficulty expressing themselves, or just need a little more probing before the light bulb goes on. As mentioned above, save the higher-level questioning—extension or reflective questions—for the left side of the notebook to help students engage in metacognitive thinking and learning.

One way to improve your questioning skills is to review student responses. Are they what you were looking for? Sometimes, all that is needed is to change one or two words. Think about whether the question is a higher- or lower-level question. Choose questions that focus on probing for student understanding. If the answer is only one or two words, change the question to require a more thorough response. The best questions allow students to think, and they help you assess whether the students are grasping the concept. Scaffold your questions to allow for self-discovery.

Work with a colleague, and try questions out on each other. One of you can role-play the student, and the other the teacher, and then you can switch roles to brainstorm possible student responses to your preplanned questions. This can help guide your lesson and identify potential problem areas.

Incorporating this type of questioning into the activity planned for the right side of the interactive notebook fits perfectly with the engage and explore phases of the 5E Learning Cycle. I *engage* the students with a key question that introduces the concept for the day. This question is written in a way that gets students to think about a problem. The question is also designed to elicit prior knowledge and any misconceptions students may have. The students write their response to the question on their own, and then they share with a partner. Next, we share ideas as a whole class, and then I allow students to add to what they originally wrote. The *explore* portion of the lesson occurs as the students complete the lab, which is embedded with more questions and activities that promote scientific inquiry. At the end of the lesson, we always revisit the key question to see if we have evidence that may support our ideas about the original problem. We discuss the evidence as a class to come to some sort of consensus about our ideas.

ELABORATE AND EXTEND: A CLOSER LOOK AT THE OUTPUT PAGE

Student work related to the elaborate and extend phase is shown on left-side notebook pages, also known as output pages. On these pages, students take the knowledge gained during the engage and explore activities and use this knowledge in new situations or real-life applications to make meaning for themselves. On these pages, I expect students to show metacognitive processing—sometimes defined as "thinking about their thinking." My goal for these pages is to help students become purposeful thinkers and independent learners, able to take control of their own learning.

Most output activities are homework assignments because I want to know if the students are internalizing and understanding concepts and not just getting answers from the group work and class discussions. I like using the left-side pages because this work is an extension of the teacher-guided, right-side pages. The left-side page provides a designated area for students to plot ongoing ideas and express their own unique thinking as they complete work on the right-side pages. They can spin off their spontaneous ideas to the left side while the original triggers remain visible on the right. This is not to say that the output page is always free-form. I assign specific work for this page, making sure it offers students an opportunity for metacognitive thinking. I find designating a specific page for metacognitive work helpful as I plan instruction. This forces me to think about what I will ask the students to do to ensure they use higher-level thinking skills in every lesson. Examples of activities for the left side include homework questions, self-reflection, graphs, data tables, and graphic organizers.

METACOGNITIVE THINKING

Interactive notebooks can provide opportunities for students to increasingly engage in metacognitive thinking. Swartz and Perkins (1989) identified four levels of thinking. At the first level, called *tacit use,* the student is thinking subconsciously, without really thinking about it. During the second level of thinking, called *aware use,* the student is conscious of his or her thoughts and actions. When engaged in the third level, *strategic use,* the student consciously organizes his or her thinking. Finally, when working at the fourth level, called *reflective use,* the student is highly aware of his or her thoughts throughout the process and reflects upon how to proceed and improve.

By orchestrating opportunities for students to progress through these phases, you will be helping students become reflective learners who can analyze and organize their thinking. To facilitate this, model your own thinking processes, and ask questions that will prompt your students to openly analyze their thoughts, bringing them to a conscious or awareness level. Write summary statements together (at the end of each lab), and provide time for students to discuss their learning with partners and the class. If you train students to listen to each other, they will feed off what other students say, and they will generate new ideas. This is very time consuming, but thinking takes time—time to process your own thoughts, and time to process what others are thinking. You can also show students how to use specific strategies or provide them with prompts to help organize their thoughts and then reflect on their learning. The following figures show examples of students organizing, analyzing, and reflecting on their learning. Figures 4.8 and 4.9 illustrate how one student organized her thoughts to make meaning.

When students are provided with teacher feedback and given opportunities to consider how to improve and revise their thinking, they are engaging in strategic and reflective levels of thought. Teacher feedback can be given at any time, but it is particularly useful when you are trying to move students toward increased levels of metacognitive thinking. Along with teacher feedback, metacognitive thinking is promoted by asking students to write a revised answer to the key question, write summary statements, or apply their understanding to new situations. If you provide ample opportunities for students to reflect on the work they do, and give them time to ask questions, revise their thinking, and apply their thinking, they will begin to ask their own questions about the work being done in class and will develop deeper understandings of their work.

Figure 4.8 The student writes notes to herself about what is happening during an interaction with riding a bike. She then formulates questions that force her to focus in on her claim and provide evidence to back her claim up.

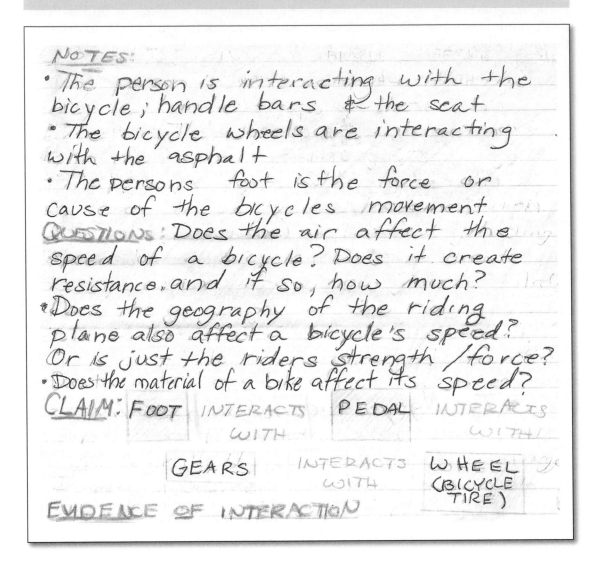

NOTES:
- The person is interacting with the bicycle; handle bars & the seat
- The bicycle wheels are interacting with the asphalt
- The persons foot is the force or cause of the bicycles movement

QUESTIONS: Does the air affect the speed of a bicycle? Does it create resistance, and if so, how much?
- Does the geography of the riding plane also affect a bicycle's speed? Or is just the riders strength / force?
- Does the material of a bike affect its speed?

CLAIM: FOOT INTERACTS PEDAL INTERACTS WITH WITH

GEARS INTERACTS WHEEL WITH (BICYCLE TIRE)

EVIDENCE OF INTERACTION

Figure 4.9 Next, the student uses pictures and diagrams to make further meaning. Throughout the process, this student uses note taking, the formulation of self-generated questions, and diagrams to help her learn how to identify a specific interaction in physics, which is making meaning of the things that are significant in the world around her.

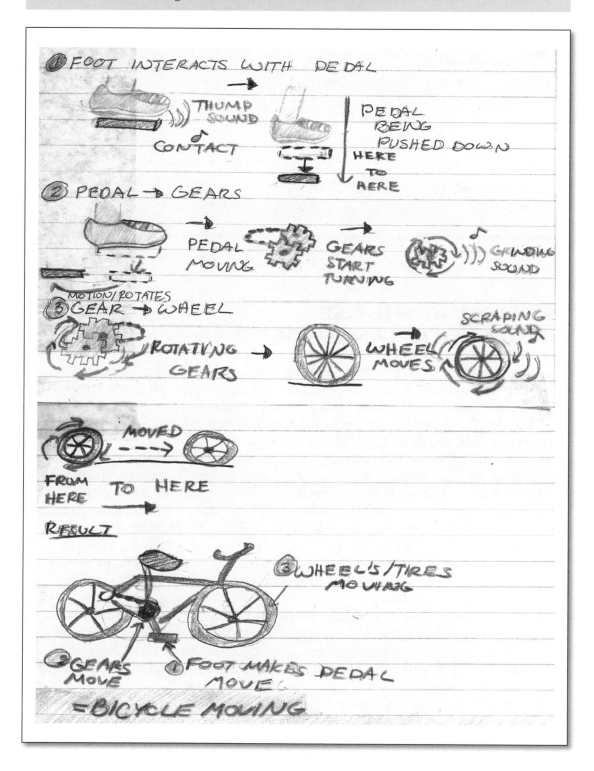

Figure 4.10   This is an example of a student writing a revised answer to a key question—an assignment at the end of almost every lesson. This student reflected on her thinking and explained exactly what she learned. The student uses key vocabulary and an example (the rubber band) to help explain her understanding.

(REVISED KEY)
Stored elastic energy increases in the elastic object when it is stretched or compressed. The further it is stretched or compressed, the more energy will be transferred when it is released. When the elastic object is released, it returns to its original shape, the stored elastic energy is changed to other types of energy such as motion energy. This can also be true for the reverse.

PROMOTING THE USE OF SCIENTIFIC LANGUAGE

Students should be using scientific language both in their written work and in conversation. To facilitate this, I use scientific-language cards. Students create these cards using colored 3" x 4" cards that correspond to the word wall created in class.

Although the scientific-language cards are created by students, they use teacher-generated words and definitions. The cards support the learning of new vocabulary as students are expected to use these words when they are writing in their interactive notebooks and when responding to questions or discussions during class. Students also use the cards to support themselves when they are trying to make connections to new ideas. Last, the cards are a useful study tool for exams. Students can quiz each other by using them as flash cards or by playing games, such as Concentration.

The front of each card shows a scientific term (key word), phonetic spelling, a picture that represents the word, a definition, and connecting words.

- The key term, placed in the upper left-hand corner is generated by the teacher, as is the definition. If you allow students to generate their own definition, you will get incorrect terminology because so many scientific terms cross over and have multiple meanings. The scientific language will be unusable if the definition is incorrect.
- Phonetic spelling is personal. It is intended to help students pronounce the word correctly, so I allow the students to generate it. I give the pronunciation, and they phonetically represent it; there is no right or wrong way; it is whatever works for them. This is particularly good for students to whom English is a second language.

Figure 4.11   The unit-one cards are yellow, the unit-two cards are green, and so on. The students' scientific-language cards are the same corresponding colors.

- The picture and connection words are also student generated; it is real neat to see what they come up with to represent the new words. If you do it for them, students will lose some sense of pride and creativity; plus, this is how they begin to learn the word, so it is important to give them the opportunity to think and process instead of just copying what the teacher did. These elements of the scientific-language cards are also great for the second-language learner, although it helps all students.

The back of the scientific-language card contains a sentence that uses the new term. The students are expected to generate a sentence that uses the word in the context of what we did in class, for example, the lab or another class activity.

When constructing scientific-language cards, try not to overwhelm the students with too many terms at one time. Decide during your planning what new words you want to introduce for a particular lesson. I typically introduce anywhere from three to five new words a week. I introduce the words on Monday, and expect completion of the cards by Friday or the following Monday, depending on the week's workload. Although I generate the words, and I almost always give the definition, occasionally I want the students to learn about a term on their own. For example, when the word was *matter*, I allowed students to construct their own definition because understanding matter is part of the targeted concept. In this case, I would give the students the word and tell them that, as a class, we will come up with a working definition for

Figure 4.12   The Elements on the Front of a Scientific-Language Card

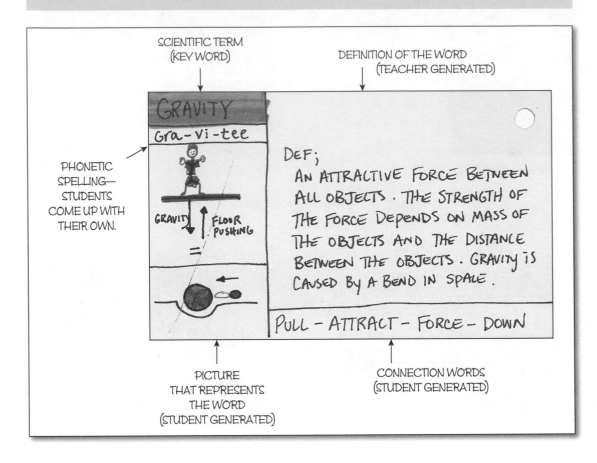

matter as we learn more about its properties. I would then plan a time during the week, and after several activities, to come to consensus as a class about the definition.

My students punch a hole in the upper right-hand corner of each card and use a large ring to keep all the cards together. Some students tape a large envelope onto the back cover of the interactive notebook and keep the cards in that. It can get bulky, and they are easy to loose track of, so another suggestion is to keep folders in the classroom for students and store all key cards in the classroom. Choosing a storage method and sticking with it is important to ensure students know what to do with their cards.

Creating scientific-language cards can be time consuming, so model the construction of the cards in the beginning of the year, and by mid-October, you can begin assigning them for homework. Grades for the cards are given at the end of each unit. I give the grades for the first unit myself, and the cards for the rest of the units are peer graded. Scientific-language cards are a very useful tool to reinforce the learning, but I don't need to spend hours grading them. I made a class chart where the students indicate whether particular cards were completed, and they grade each other.

Figure 4.13 The Back of a Scientific-Language Card. Students make connections from the new vocabulary to the concepts learned in class.

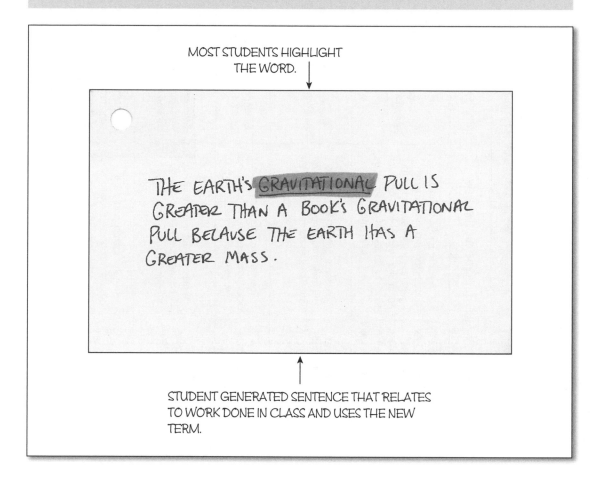

A CONTINUUM OF TEACHER-STUDENT INTERACTIVITY

The National Research Council identified the following essential features of classroom inquiry: engagement in scientifically oriented questions; use of evidence when responding to questions; formulating explanations from evidence; connecting evidence to scientific knowledge; and communicating and justifying explanations (National Research Council, 2000).

During a professional-development conference, I was part of a group of teachers who developed a continuum for student notebooks showing levels of teacher and student interactivity applied to these features of classroom inquiry. Figure 4.14 shows the continuum we developed. The columns on the left of the continuum reflect greater levels of teacher-directed instruction, while the columns on the right of the continuum reflect more student independence in the learning processes. Teachers can review student notebooks and determine whether the student-written

Figure 4.14 Essential Features of Notebook Interactivity. As you can see below, in the thinking category, on the more teacher-guided side, the teacher would generate the thinking behind the purpose and move into shared instruction (e.g., writing frames and think alouds). Then, slowly move into the shared instruction column where the teacher and student interact to explore concepts, and the teacher might use something like sentence frames to help the student. Moving toward the metacognitive side of thinking, the teacher is just there as a guide for the student when the student explores the concepts, and the teacher might use something like a word bank to help guide the student. Until, finally, you move to the independent side where the student initiates his or her own thinking and explains how things work using his or her own words.

(Mostly found on the right side of the interactive notebook)   *(Mostly found on the left side of the interactive notebook)*

WHO IS DOING THE…	TEACHER-GUIDED INSTRUCTION	SHARED INSTRUCTION	GUIDE ON THE SIDE	INDEPENDENT INSTRUCTION
QUESTIONING	Teacher poses questions for students. (predetermined questions and answers)	Teacher and students both pose questions. Teacher has an end result in mind to arrive at the ESR. (questions from which to choose, answers are predetermined)	Teacher poses the initial question and the students generate the remainder of the questions. (higher-level question leads to additional questions by students)	Students pose their own questions and may or may not attempt to answer them.
CITING EVIDENCE	Teacher demonstrates and points out evidence of how something works. Students duplicate evidence. (data table, pictures, arrows, demos)	Teacher cites significant meaning in the data, and with help the students generate evidence.	Students generate, organize, and make meaning of their own data. Teacher guides them in the process.	Students are responsible for identifying evidence and making meaning of it.
EXPLAINS	Teacher generates and models explanations of how things work.	Teacher leads students' explanations with a goal in mind.	Teacher prompts students to dictate explanations of how things work. (teacher questioning)	Students can explain in words or drawings "how things work."
THINKING	Teacher generates the thinking behind the purpose, and the students duplicate in the notebook. (e.g., writing frames, think alouds)	Teacher and students interact as students explore the concept. (e.g., sentence frames)	Teacher initiates the thinking, and the students explore the concept. (e.g., word bank)	Students initiate thinking. (i.e., the students explain how things work in their own words)
MAKES CONNECTIONS	Teacher identifies connections/relationships by pointing them out.	Teacher asks questions that lead to connections that are present in the students' notebooks.	Students identify and clarify a possible connection/ relationship in the notebooks. Small amount of teacher guidance. Teacher may coach/prompt to initiate process.	Students are able to identify connections/relationships by articulating and using evidence for support from within the notebook.
DETERMINES MODE OF COMMUNICATION	Teacher determines type of output product.	Teacher and students discuss and determine the output together.	Teacher minimally guides students to produce.	Students generate output independently.

Teacher ──────► Student

Amount of Instruction/Direction

Essential Processing Feature

70

evidence on a particular page reflects more teacher-guided work or more independent student work. This is not to say that one is better or more effective than the other, it is merely one means of identifying whether the work the students are doing (as reflected in the notebooks) needs to move more in either direction. For example, if students need more modeling to understand a concept, then you know you can design more shared-instruction experiences. However, if evidence from the notebooks shows solid understanding of a key concept, you can probably move toward more independent instruction.

Thus, the continuum can be used two ways—as both an evaluative guide and as a planning guide for interactive notebooks. Teachers may use it to evaluate what students are doing and how students are processing the work they do, especially when it comes to applying concepts to new ideas. The continuum can also be used to spark your own thinking processes about the work students are doing. At any time during the year, you can decide to incorporate either more teacher-guided or more student-generated work, and you can use the guide to help plan instruction and design the individual notebook pages.

SUMMARY

The right side of the notebook, which incorporates the engage, explore, and naturally interwoven evaluation portion of the 5Es, is the teacher-facilitated section and is filled with questions, self-discovery, and inquiry. If you look at a student's notebook on the right side, you should get an understanding of their thinking process throughout the lesson. The left-side, or output, pages are where you integrate metacognition or higher-level thinking into each lesson. When constructing the input and output pages, remember

- The properties of a lab should include elements of experimental design that fit in a 5E model;
- Develop good questions for the purpose of probing for student understanding and guiding student learning;
- Use scientific language and key questions as learning tools;
- Give students ample opportunities to reflect on their learning;
- Assign output pages for homework to get a better idea of how students are internalizing the concepts; and
- Be aware of the continuum of interactivity in the notebooks, from teacher-guided to student-generated work, and make adjustments as needed.

5

Getting Started

The First Three Days

I n the previous chapters, we have explored how notebooks are used in the science classroom to facilitate student learning. This chapter will explain the nuts and bolts of the first three days of notebooking—how to organize and execute the process, how to manage the time it takes to construct notebooks, and what to do each day with students.

Whenever I find myself talking to a teacher who wants to implement interactive notebooks in his or her classroom, a common question is, "How do I get it started?" My answer is always, "By starting!" However, I understand that what many teachers find helpful is a step-by-step process. In this chapter, I will provide the "how-tos" day by day. I explain exactly what I do on the first day of school and so on. I have followed this process for several years without much variation.

This is what works best for me, and I encourage you to take from my experience what you believe will work best for you. Follow my process exactly, or take bits and pieces, formatting it to fit your own style of teaching. My goal is to give you a glimpse into my classroom and explain how I implement interactive notebooks in a manner that works effectively for my students. If you are beginning notebooking for the first time, know that this is one teacher's practice you may want to try. If you have been using interactive notebooks for a while, you may find some new ideas and ways that may help improve your own practice. I have confidence in my process because when I follow these basic procedures, I get sustained student use and quality in-depth student work. That's not to say that if you do exactly what I do in the first week you will have perfect students with beautiful notebooks. Effective notebooking takes time, patience, and practice. However, if you practice some of the strategies that are outlined here, I believe you will see great gains in your student buy in, work quality, and learning.

CHOOSING THE NOTEBOOKS

I recommend using spiral notebooks without perforated pages if you can find them; those with 70 pages work best. One year, I tried using loose-leaf paper in a binder but students kept losing the pages, forgetting to put the pages in the binder, or mixing up the order. It was a big mess. A 70-page notebook is nice because it seems to just fit the year. Students will be using both sides of the page, so you get 140 pages. I have used more than 70 pages twice, but it was no big deal to start a new notebook; by the end of the first semester, most students want to start a new book anyway. (I never let them). It's hard to keep students from starting over as they get better and better and more conscientious about their work. Try getting them to understand that seeing their own progression over time is beneficial, and it shows their learning and growth over the year. Explain to them that, in a sense, they are writing their own science textbook that documents the year's learning. Convey to them that it will be something that they can continue to look back on just like a real text. It will be a constant reminder of the rules, rubrics, and prior evidence that will help guide them to the next discovery. It is a learning flow that will also help the teacher assess their understanding throughout the year. Remind students that real scientists keep journals, and they can practice the same protocols and procedures that scientists use.

DAY ONE

Introducing the Notebooks

Day one is a short pep talk and introduction to the idea of notebooks. Show examples of the prior year's notebooks if you have them. First, I show examples of cover pages, graphics, color, and organizational ideas. This helps establish my expectations and is far more interesting than reading a class syllabus. Then, I introduce the idea of homework, telling students that they have homework on the first day of school. (It's easy, but they don't know that yet). They complain a little, but inside most students love to go home on the first day and say, "School is so hard, I have homework on the first day." The homework is numbering all 70 notebook pages, front and back, starting from page 1 to page 140. This means that they need to be careful not to skip any pages or repeat any numbers. Remind students not to tear any pages out of the notebook at any time! If a mistake is made, the student will have to fix it on the existing page and move on. I tell them to number the pages in black or blue ink (no erasable ink and no fancy colors). They should number the pages on the bottom right hand corner of the right-side page, and the bottom left hand corner of the left-side page. All right-side pages will be odd numbers, and all left-side pages will be even numbers. This way, when you or the students are looking for a particular page, all you have to do is thumb through the bottom corner of the notebook pages.

Figure 5.1   This shows where to place the numbers, on the outside lower corner of the pages. Remind students that numbers are on the outside edges of each page in the notebook, not near the spiral.

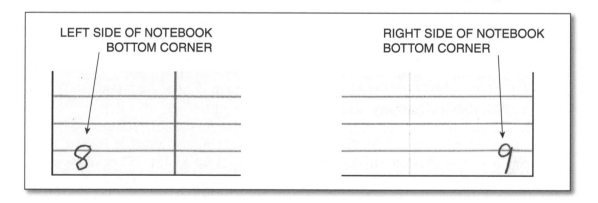

You can demonstrate by turning the pages and showing them how to number each page. They tell me what number goes on which page as I go. Do this for five or six pages. They think it's silly until the next day when you find several of the students who have made errors or didn't do it at all. Page numbers become the first graded project for the year. The next morning, the moment they come in the classroom, we grade the homework that they completed. I will explain more about how I do that on day two.

Numbering the Pages

So, why do I set the pages up in the beginning, and why like this? Throughout the year, I will ask my students to do specific work on specific pages. When I say turn to pages 60 and 61, I want all students at the same place at the same time, especially when we are looking back on prior days' work to make meaning of it during a current lesson. (I will tell you about flip pages later, which are implemented when a student has more to say and they run out of room to say it on a given page.) We number both sides of each page so that we can utilize the entire interactive notebook just like a real book. We number all pages the first day because if we don't students will forget to number as they go, and then you and the student will lose track of pages. We use permanent ink for obvious reasons: The numbers need to last all year without getting erased. This facilitates grading because all students are on the same page, and I can grade every student's notebook by looking for specific pages. Or, I can say, "You are missing the work on pages 22 and 23." We also keep a table of contents on the inside front cover of the notebook that tracks all the assignments with page titles and numbers. (I will talk about titles and dates later. Also, you will find a reproducible Table of Contents page in the Resources section at the end of this book.) Figure 5.2 shows a sample of what a student's table of contents might look like.

The distribution of notebooks, display of past samples, and assignment of page numbering should take about 10 minutes of class time.

Labeling the Cover

Next, we label the front cover of the notebook by using a permanent marker. I have about 120 to 240 students a year, and it is very important to keep track of student notebooks by class and grade level. In class, students label the front cover of their notebooks with their names (first and last), science class period, grade, date, and teacher name. This way, if another teacher finds the notebook laying around in another class, they can see my name and put it in my box.

I should mention that of all the years I have been using interactive notebooks, about two students a year lose their work. Students understand that we use them every day and that their grade depends on keeping it up to date. They also realize that if they lose it they will need to recreate a new one using my teacher notebook, which is no fun. It is loads of extra work for being unorganized, and they know it, so they work very hard to never lose sight of their notebooks. That includes letting another student borrow it. Most students just won't take the risk of giving up their books for any reason. I have to actually bribe students to let me use their notebooks for workshops. It isn't pretty: I have created notebook fanatics.

Labeling the notebooks will take another 5 minutes of class time. The rest of the class period is up to you. It will take around 15 minutes altogether to introduce interactive notebooks on the first day.

> **Figure 5.2** Students organize the table of contents by page title and number. It is divided into two columns that correspond to the left and right sides of the notebook. All even numbers are on the left, and all odd numbers are located on the right. The unit title is at the top. We use a new table of contents for each new unit to make it easy to find specific pages.

Table of Contents for Your Interactive Notebook

Name _____   Unit Title Interactions & Forces

Left Side	Page	Right Side	Page
Pushes & Pulls Around Us	56	Balloon Puck Lab	57
Practice Diagrams	58	Pushes, Pulls, Motion	59
Your Own Frictionless World	60		

Total Number of Assignments Completed in this Unit _____

Figure 5.3 This is a sample of the front cover of the interactive notebook. Large labels make it easy to see which student the notebook belongs to, and the labels are organizational aids when you collect all the notebooks at the same time. You can sort them by period this way as well. Felt-tip permanent marker works best because the ink will last all year.

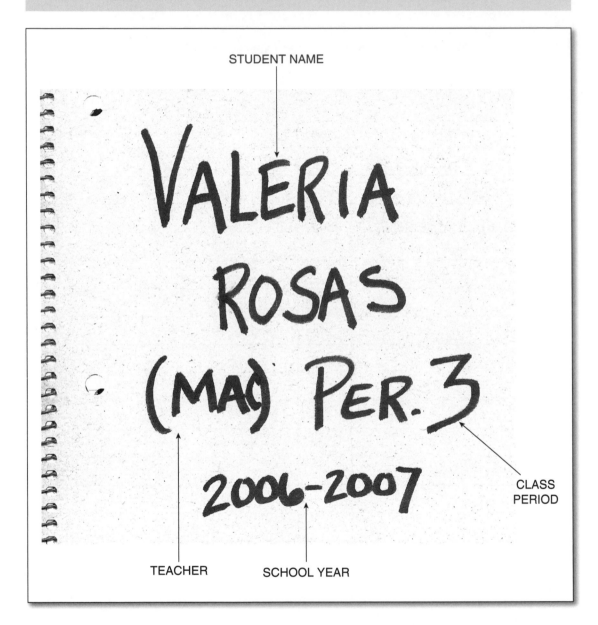

On day one, I like to end the class with a group team-building activity. This gives the students an idea of how I expect them to work together as a team throughout the year. It generates group participation and discussion (which they will be engaging in daily), and let's face it, it's fun! This is a great way to end the class because they are pumped up and happy about science as well as motivated to do their homework. This positive attitude helps to get everyone in the right frame of mind for the new school year.

DAY TWO

Homework Expectations and Grading

As soon as the students sit down, I start talking about the homework. I tell them that I will be coming around the class in 5 minutes to check the completion of the assignment and record the grade as their first science grade. This sets the tone for accountability. Students know that I mean business and that I plan to check all their work in a timely manner. I check the notebooks everyday for the next week and a half to reinforce this. This is often a simple spot check to see which students I might need to focus on with regard to follow through. Students usually understand my expectations by day three.

I ask the students to trade notebooks and check every page of their partner's notebook (peer grading). This takes approximately five minutes; and while they are peer grading, I walk around and troubleshoot. I talk to the students who wrote the numbers in the wrong spot, skipped a page, didn't finish, and so on. I deliver the bad news that they need to fix the problem and make the notebook right. For some students, this will be a lot of extra work, but you can bet that for the next homework assignment, they will be listening very closely and follow all instructions properly. The students who did not finish will be writing frantically, which is appropriate because they are getting the work done. Their grade, however, will reflect the unfinished work.

Some students may become upset that they missed an opportunity to get full credit, so I talk to the class about makeup work, explaining that all work can be made up. Students can go back and change things, add to written work, and so on, especially after a class discussion. I strongly encourage this in the beginning, and I always give a minute or two for the students to reflect on their learning and decide if they want to modify what they wrote in their notebooks. Even after several weeks, students may decide to go back and finish work, or add to work that they have already completed. I allow this because I am not going to argue with a student who wants to improve on their work by reflecting on their learning. I always allow students to make up grades, not always for full credit, but close. (They think this is great and don't realize that they are actually learning by going back and reflecting on the work they did.) It also helps them with making connections from day to day because they are reviewing prior days' work. They learn follow-through by starting something and eventually taking it from beginning to end.

If by the third day I have a student that has not completed two assignments in a row, I inform them that we will be making a phone call home to notify his or her parents that it has been only three days since school has started and their daughter or son is already missing two assignments. (And easy assignments at that!) I explain this in class so that all students understand the consequences before phone calls begin on day three. It usually takes only one or two students per class before the students realize I mean what I say. (This technique is especially important in the upper-grade levels.) The students quickly learn that apathy and laziness are not options in my class. This puts the ownership on them; they have choices to make and are responsible for their own learning. This helps each student internalize the idea that "I, the student, am responsible for the work I do. I want to learn and do well in class, so I need to follow some simple guidelines: follow procedures, participate in class and group discussions, respect others and myself, be prepared for class, (with an up-to-date notebook), search for answers to my many questions by exploring, talking, testing, researching, and so on."

Keep a list of student names (you might want to use a simple class roster for this at the beginning), and record all grades on that list for the first week. Walk from table to table asking students to report on the peer grading and whether the work was complete or incomplete, and record the appropriate grade (full credit, half credit, or no credit). Tell them at that moment what grade they received and why. Again, you are establishing expectations. Students begin to realize that feedback will be offered in a timely manner, and you will be conferring with them about the their work.

> The peer page-number grading and class chat should take approximately 10 minutes of class time.

The First Eight Pages

The next step is to hand out the first eight pages, which will be placed in the notebook, and the table of contents, which is placed on the inside of the front cover. The first eight pages are packed with information to guide students and parents in the use of interactive notebooks. (Reproducibles for these may be found in the Resource A section).

> **The First Eight Pages**
> 1. Interactive Notebook Rubric
> 2. Aha Connections Visual Outline
> 3. Words of Wisdom About the Aha Connections Visual Outline
> 4. Why We Keep Interactive Notebooks in Science
> 5. Interactive Notebook Thinking Processes
> 6. Constructing the Aha Connections Pages
> 7. How to Write an Aha Connections Thesis
> 8. How to Write a Self-Reflection

These eight handouts need to be cut and trimmed then taped onto the appropriate pages in the notebook. I use only scotch tape because white glue soaks in and warps the pages, glue sticks won't last (the pages fall out only days later), and staples rip the pages. Take my word for this, I have tried them all and tape is your best bet. Buy lots of tape during the holiday season to stock up, and ask students to help out a little when they can.

Cutting and taping is a homework assignment. (Since it is usually the second day of school, most parents will consider the tape and scissors school supplies, and if they do not already have them at home, they will make a point to get them for home use.) I explain to students that just like a real text, the beginning of the notebook is filled with important information about what you will find within the pages of the interactive notebook. I briefly go over each handout by title and ask the students to write, at the top or on the backside of the handout, the number of the notebook page it should be taped on. There is no need to go in depth about what is on each page because that will be part of the homework.

The homework for the evening is to read each page and highlight, color, and underline key points. Students are to write down any questions that they may have on a sticky note and come prepared the next morning for a class discussion about the topics of each page. Remind students that the homework grade will be based on all pages being cut, trimmed, and taped onto the correct corresponding page in the interactive notebook. Each page must contain highlights or key components outlined in some way. And each student must come prepared the next morning with questions or comments about the pages. Explain that students should make sure that there are no loose pages and that nothing is hanging over the pages in the notebook. If you give a notebook the "shake test," nothing should fall out. If you close the notebook, you should see nothing but the cover without any papers hanging out. While this may seem obsessive, I have found that it helps ensure that the notebooks will last all year. Also, this reinforces my expectation of neatness.

> Passing out the first eight pages and going over homework expectations will take approximately 10 minutes. Total time spent on notebooks for day two is approximately 20 minutes.

DAY THREE

Day three is intense, as you will be addressing a number of key topics—notebook expectations, labels, dates, and the table of contents—and assigning the cover page as homework. To prepare you to answer students' questions, let's begin by examining the first eight pages.

Page One: Interactive Notebook Rubric

Page one (right side) is the Interactive Notebook Rubric. It outlines notebook expectations on a number scale from 5 to 10, with 10 being best. The rubric ensures that students and parents alike know what the teacher is looking for in student work. No one should be surprised by the grades earned. Figure 5.4 shows the rubric.

At the end of every unit, students write a self-reflection paper. Students use the rubric to rate the work they have completed thus far in their interactive notebook. Periodically, I ask the parents to grade the notebook at home and send a signed notice back to school with the rating; they use the rubric for that as well. This keeps the parents informed of their students' progress and puts the responsibility back on the student. Parents like this because it gives them something to talk about with their child. Since it's an easy grade, students will do it, and when parents ask, "What did you do in school today?" they won't hear the usual, "Nothing." All they have to do is pick up the notebook, read, and discuss.

You may find that you receive fewer parent complaints because your expectations are clear from the start. At a parent conference, you can open the notebook, look at the rubric, and say, "Based on the rubric, how do you think Tommy is doing?" The expectations are right there.

Figure 5.4   To earn a 10, the notebook should reflect in-depth understanding of concepts learned. These students go over and above what is asked of them. They draw, write, ask questions, and reflect throughout the notebook in places where the teacher had no such expectation. A 9 is almost a 10 but without the over and above. Both a 9 and 10 reflect an "A student's" work. The 7 notebook is your borderline student. With some conferring and direction, this student can easily move from a 7 to an 8. When you get the 5 notebook, you don't have much to work with, but the opportunity for improvement is huge!

Interactive Notebook Rubric

10	**"Totally Awesome" (Almost Gross)** The writing goes beyond the basic requirements and shows in-depth understanding of concepts. The work shows in-depth reflection throughout the learning process. Your notebook has all the components expected, including dates and labels on each page. All pages are numbered properly with odd numbers on the right and even numbers on the left. Right- and left-side work is correctly organized with all criteria. The use of color and labeled diagrams enhance understanding. The notebook is so tidy it's almost "gross!"
9	**"Awesome"** The writing follows the basic requirements, shows understanding of concepts, but does not go beyond. The work shows in-depth reflection. Your notebook has all the components expected, including dates and labels on each page. All pages are numbered properly with odd numbers on the right and even numbers on the left. Right- and left-side work is correctly organized with all criteria. The notebook has color, and the student uses labeled diagrams. A "9" looks much like a "10," but it lacks the "totally" in "awesome."
8	**"Pretty Darn Good"** The written work shows a basic understanding of concepts. An honest reflection, but limited. Your notebook has about 90% of the components expected, with dates and labels. All pages are numbered properly with odd numbers on the right and even numbers on the left. Right- and left-side work is correctly organized. The notebook has some color and diagrams, with a few labels. Some requirements are met, but your notebook lacks criteria in all areas.
7	**"Kick It Up a Notch"** The written work shows a limited understanding of concepts. Limited reflection overall. Your notebook has about 80% of the components expected, with dates and labels. Most pages are numbered. Right- and left-side work is fairly organized, "just so-so." The notebook has very little color and hardly any diagrams. Notebook components are rarely met.
6	**"Better Get Movin'"** The written work shows misconceptions and a lack of understanding. "Reflection, what reflection?" The pages in your notebook are unfinished. You tried, but the dates and labels did not make it to the page. There are inconsistencies in your right- and left-side entries. The notebook is unorganized, and "the dog ate your pages."
5	**"What Were You Thinking?"** Hey, you turned in a notebook, but the pages are blank, or they include the class template only. "Maybe you wrote with invisible ink?"

Pages Two and Three: Aha Connections Visual Outline and Words of Wisdom About the Aha Connections Visual Outline

Page two (left side) is the Aha Connections Visual Outline. (See Figure 5.5.) This corresponds with page three (right side), Words of Wisdom About the Aha Connections Visual Outline. (See Figure 5.6.) These two pages explain the main concept behind the interactive notebook, which is to give opportunity to students to gather information from many sources in order to critically answer scientific problems. What you find on the pages within the interactive notebook are the lines of evidence that support or refute scientific ideas.

Pages Four and Five: Why We Keep Interactive Notebooks in Science and Interactive Notebook Thinking Processes

Page four (left side) is an outline for students and parents about why we use interactive notebooks, what to expect, and what types of assignments go on the right and left sides of pages. Figure 5.7 shows this page, which introduces the idea of metacognition—the higher-level thinking that students will be doing throughout the year.

Students are expected to use the information from the right side of their notebooks to make meaning and then show their understanding of these new concepts on the left side of their notebooks by presenting it in a new way using their own style. Page five (right side) is a visual organizer to help with this understanding. (See Figure 5.8.) I believe it is important to keep students informed of expectations and the reasons for using the right-side–left-side format. These pages also serve as a handy reminder to students about what type of activities are shown on the right- and left-side pages. (I don't usually go into too much detail about metacognition or higher-level thinking with the students. I keep the discussion at a basic level.)

Pages Six and Seven: Constructing the Aha Connections Pages and How to Write an Aha Connections Thesis

Page six (left side) shows how to construct the Aha Connections pages, where students record the summary statements they write at the end of each investigation. Details about how to construct these pages with students were outlined in Chapter 2.

Page seven (right side) is How to Write an Aha Connections Thesis. You don't want to scare the students, but they need to know that you have high expectations for student writing in your science class. Scientists document the work they do, and the student scientists in your class will do the same. Express to your students that when the time comes, you will go over all expectations of how to write an aha thesis and model the process for them. This handout will be placed on page seven of their interactive notebook for future use. More information about writing the aha thesis is in Chapter 7.

Page Eight: How to Write a Self-Reflection

Page eight (left side) explains how to write a self-reflection paper. At the end of every unit, I ask my students to write a paper that reflects on the work done during that unit. (This is done four to five times a year, so it is nice for the students to have

Figure 5.5   Aha Connections Visual Outline. I look at it in three main parts: the trigger and scientific problem, the gathering of evidence from multiple sources, and the thesis paper that supports the learning. This visual puts those ideas together in a way that is easy to understand, and the outline walks you through each component. I include these pages in the front of the interactive notebook as a way of reminding students and parents of my interactive notebook approach.

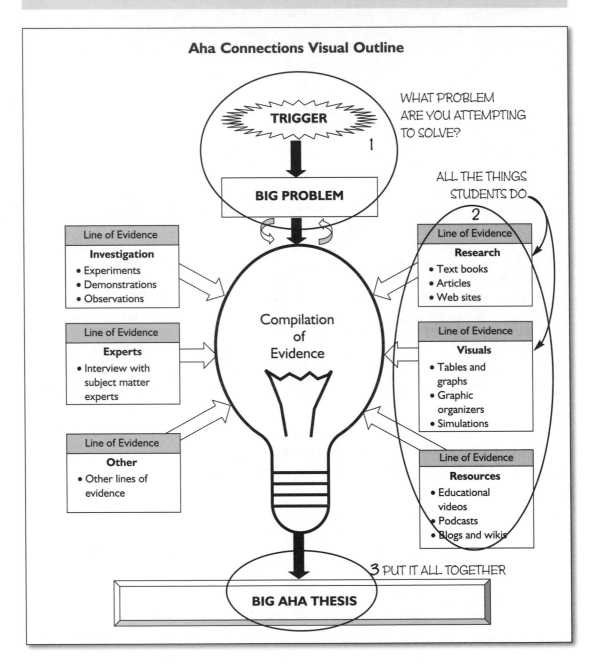

Figure 5.6   Words of Wisdom About the Aha Connections Visual Outline handout

**Words of Wisdom About
the Aha Connections Visual Outline**

Scientists gather evidence from many sources, including investigations, research, experts, visuals, and other resources. This evidence often supports and or refutes other lines of evidence. The goal of this approach to immersion and interactive notebooks is to allow students to gather information from many sources in order to critically answer scientific problems.

Trigger

A trigger is a *spark* of interest that leads students to their question or big problem. In order to allow students an opportunity to find this spark, students need to be given time to do observations. (Visual observations, asking questions, reading, watching educational videos, interviewing scientists, etc.) This provides an opportunity for buy in for all students.

Big Problem

Students think about their readings, visual observations, and so on, and start forming questions. These questions are summarized into one big problem or question that students can now investigate.

Lines of Evidence

Students can gather evidence from many sources. The rectangular boxes list these sources of evidence. Often, students of science get their evidence primarily from lab experiments; however, there are other sources that can be used to support or refute evidence found during experimentation. Lines of evidence include but are not limited to investigations, research, consulting experts, visuals, simulations, and other resources.

DRAW ARROWS
TO MAKE
CONNECTIONS

Compilation of Evidence

Students gather all lines of evidence and find connections or conflicts among pieces of information. As students are compiling this information, they may find that there are holes in their evidence and they need to do more research.

The Aha Thesis

The students take all of the evidence that they have collected and compile it into a formal writing piece. The end result should be a multiparagraph essay with an introductory paragraph, body paragraphs that summarize each line of evidence, and a closing paragraph. Students can use the lines of evidence as stems for writing their big idea thesis.

PUTTING IT ALL TOGETHER

the directions handy. (See Figure 5.9.) Otherwise, they forget, and you have to review it time and time again.) The first time students write the self-reflection paper, I go over the directions thoroughly, model the writing, and show examples of written work. After the first time, all that is needed is to refer the students to this page, tell them to use their last paper as a guide, and they can complete the assignment on their own. This is another great reason for keeping notebooks: In a non-notebook classroom, most students will have filed their self-reflection directions and past graded papers in the circular file cabinet, more commonly known as the trashcan. In the interactive notebook classroom, students can refer back to past days' work in order to grow and move forward, while making connections to past learning. Chapter 7 will go into detail about how to help students create a self-reflection paper.

Figure 5.7 Why We Keep Interactive Notebooks in Science handout. Most students will go through and highlight the key components of each handout.

Why We Keep Interactive Notebooks in Science

To keep an interactive notebook you will need:

➔ An 8 ½" × 11" spiral notebook with at least 70 pages (college ruled is preferred, and *without* perforated pages is best)
➔ Colored pencils, crayons, and highlighters
➔ Tape
➔ A small pair of scissors
➔ A pen and pencil with an eraser

BASIC SUPPLIES

You will be using your interactive notebook in class every day to help you learn new science concepts and to help you make connections to those concepts. Your interactive notebook will also help you organize your thoughts in a fun and creative way.

Left Side—Output *Even numbered pages	Right Side—Input *Odd numbered pages
The left side of the notebook is used to show your understanding of the new concepts that you are learning in class. We call this the metacognition, or higher-level thinking, side of your notebook. You will be working with the information from the right, input, side and presenting it in your own way on this left side. We use the left side for . . .	The right side of the notebook is for your facilitated learning. This side is mostly used for the work that you do in class with your teacher and with other classmates. We have a lot of conversations and questions that we try to answer. You will be recording that work on this, right, side of your notebook. We use the right side for . . .
✖ Your questions	✖ Key questions
✖ Brainstorming diagrams	✖ Hypotheses
✖ Making connections	✖ Procedures
✖ Graphing	✖ Labs/Observations
✖ Summary/Conclusions	✖ Data
✖ Applying what you know to the real world/Big Idea	✖ Key words/Notes/Class consensus ideas

Figure 5.8 Interactive Notebook Thinking Processes handout. This page has a dual purpose: It is easy to understand, and it promotes student buy in. When students place their own picture in the center of the page they begin to "own" the notebook. The actual placing of their picture here will be incorporated in the homework for day four.

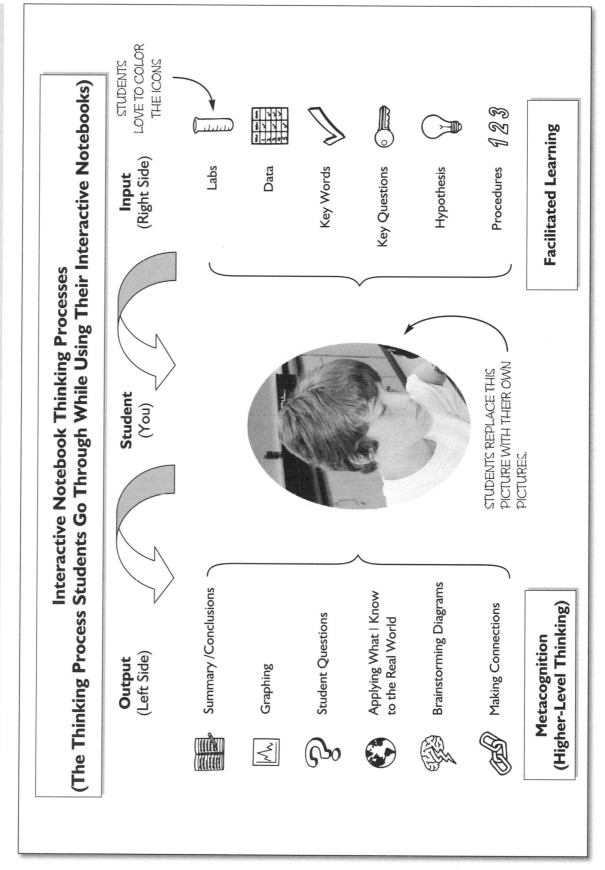

Interactive Notebook Thinking Processes
(The Thinking Process Students Go Through While Using Their Interactive Notebooks)

Output
(Left Side)

Summary /Conclusions

Graphing

Student Questions

Applying What I Know
to the Real World

Brainstorming Diagrams

Making Connections

Metacognition
(Higher-Level Thinking)

Student
(You)

STUDENTS REPLACE THIS
PICTURE WITH THEIR OWN
PICTURES.

Input
(Right Side)

STUDENTS
LOVE TO COLOR
THE ICONS

Labs

Data

Key Words

Key Questions

Hypothesis

Procedures

Facilitated Learning

Figure 5.9 How to Write a Self-Reflection handout. This walks the students through exactly what to do, paragraph by paragraph. The purpose of this activity is to give students a place where they can write their personal opinions. This assignment asks the students to be reflective and honest about the process they are engaged in. This is similar to the criteria sheet above that corresponds with writing the aha thesis.

How to Write a Self-Reflection

You will be expected to write a reflective essay at the end of each unit that shows your in-depth understanding about the work you are doing. Be honest and open in sharing your thoughts and opinions.

Step 1: Count the number of the assignments we have completed for this unit, and record it at the top of your reflection.

TIES INTO THE AHA CONNECTIONS

Step 2: Choose four pages from this unit that best supported the Big Aha in your unit thesis, two from the left side and two from the right side, and list them on your reflection below the assignment count.

Step 3: You will now be writing three paragraphs.

> **Paragraph 1:** Write specific reasons for why you chose the four assignments that you listed.

> **Paragraph 2:** Explain why these pages best support your unit thesis. Give specific examples.

> **Paragraph 3:** What do these assignments reflect about your skills as a student? For example, you may write that they show that I am organized, I am good at analyzing, I was very thorough, creative, my information was very accurate, I made connections from one assignment to another, and so on. Make sure that you cite specific examples from the pages you listed.

Step 4: This will be **Paragraph 4.** In this paragraph, you will rate your own notebook. Use the rubric to rate your work as a 10, 9, 8, 7, 6, or 5. How do you think your notebook measures up and why? Use specifics from the rubric, and relate it directly to the pages you listed. (Use examples.)

Step 5: This will be **Paragraph 5,** the last paragraph of your reflection. Hurray! Answer the following questions:

- What information did you learn that was new to you? Give specific examples.
- How did your notebook help you in this unit? Again, be specific.
- How could you improve your notebook? Please explain.

THIS IS GREAT FOR THE TEACHER TO SEE!

Please type your final draft, and tape it as a flip page in your interactive notebook as specified by your teacher.

> **Figure 5.10** All page titles are teacher generated, with the date located directly underneath. Again, remember that all titles and dates are at the top of each page, near the outside edges, not near the spine.

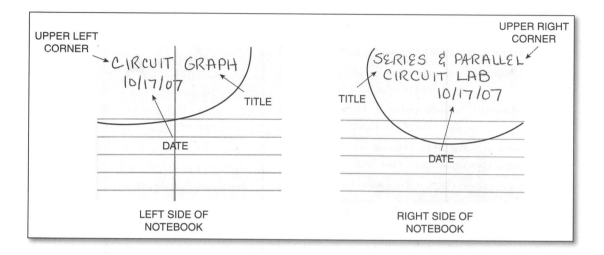

Titles, Page Labels, and Dates

After answering questions about the first eight pages, I show students how to format the titles, page labels, and dates.

Left-side pages have the page title and date in the upper left-hand corner. Right-side pages have the title and date in the upper right-hand corner, as seen in Figure 5.10.

The titles and dates serve the same purpose as the page numbers. You can finger through the pages at the top without having to open up the entire book. It's quicker, less damaging to the notebook pages, and more efficient. The truth is, the students and you will finger through the pages frequently, looking back at prior activities to make connections, revamping graphs, checking data that was previously collected, making up assignments, and grading work.

The page titles and lab names are teacher generated. I use an overhead document projector each day to show the students the page titles, dates, and page numbers, as well as prompts I expect to see on the student pages. I use my teacher notebook as a template, writing directly on it, and modeling the set up for each day. If you do not have access to an overhead document projector, you can draw a notebook template on the board showing how the student notebook should look. In the past, I have constructed a large, permanent model of a notebook on the front board using electrical tape. It looked just like a student notebook, and I used it every day. It was an effective, easy-to-follow visual for students. During the first five minutes of class, students set up the notebook pages that we will be using that day. The setup always includes a key question. The students write the prompt, answer the question in a "quick write" format, and then turn and talk to a neighbor about the key question. As a result, the first 8 to 10 minutes in class are silent with all students on task.

Figure 5.11 This shows the creation of a template on the board. Electrical tape is easy to remove and leaves minimal residue.

Figure 5.12 This shows what a template on the board might look like.

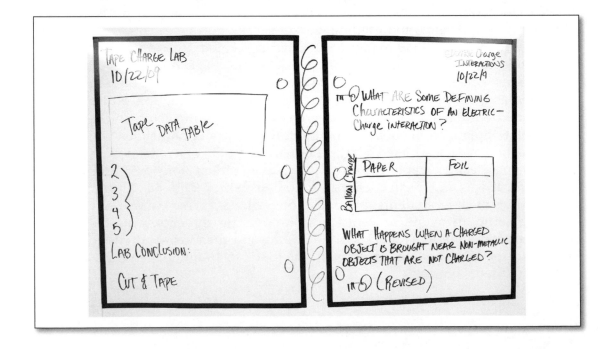

Figure 5.13 Using interactive notebooks is a compelling reason for getting an overhead document projector. The document projector is extremely useful for showing student work to the class as well as allowing students to come up and explain a finding to their peers.

The Table of Contents

After you demonstrate how to label each page with titles and dates, model for students how to record the information on their table of contents. The table of contents is taped to the inside front cover of the interactive notebook. In the beginning, you will need to remind students quite frequently to record all page information on the table of contents. I keep a large version of the table of contents on chart paper in the back of the room. While the students are responding to their key questions in the morning, I walk to the back of the room and record the new pages onto the chart paper. This serves as a prompt to the students, who upon seeing me do this, turn to the front cover of their notebooks and record the information in their own table of contents.

Figure 5.14 This is a running log of what gets recorded in a table of contents. Displaying a large version in the classroom at all times helps the students. It reminds them to keep up with their notebook and stay organized. The table of contents also helps the teacher when he or she is looking for a particular assignment and needs to know where to find it. Explain to students that real books have a table of contents, so their notebook should have one as well.

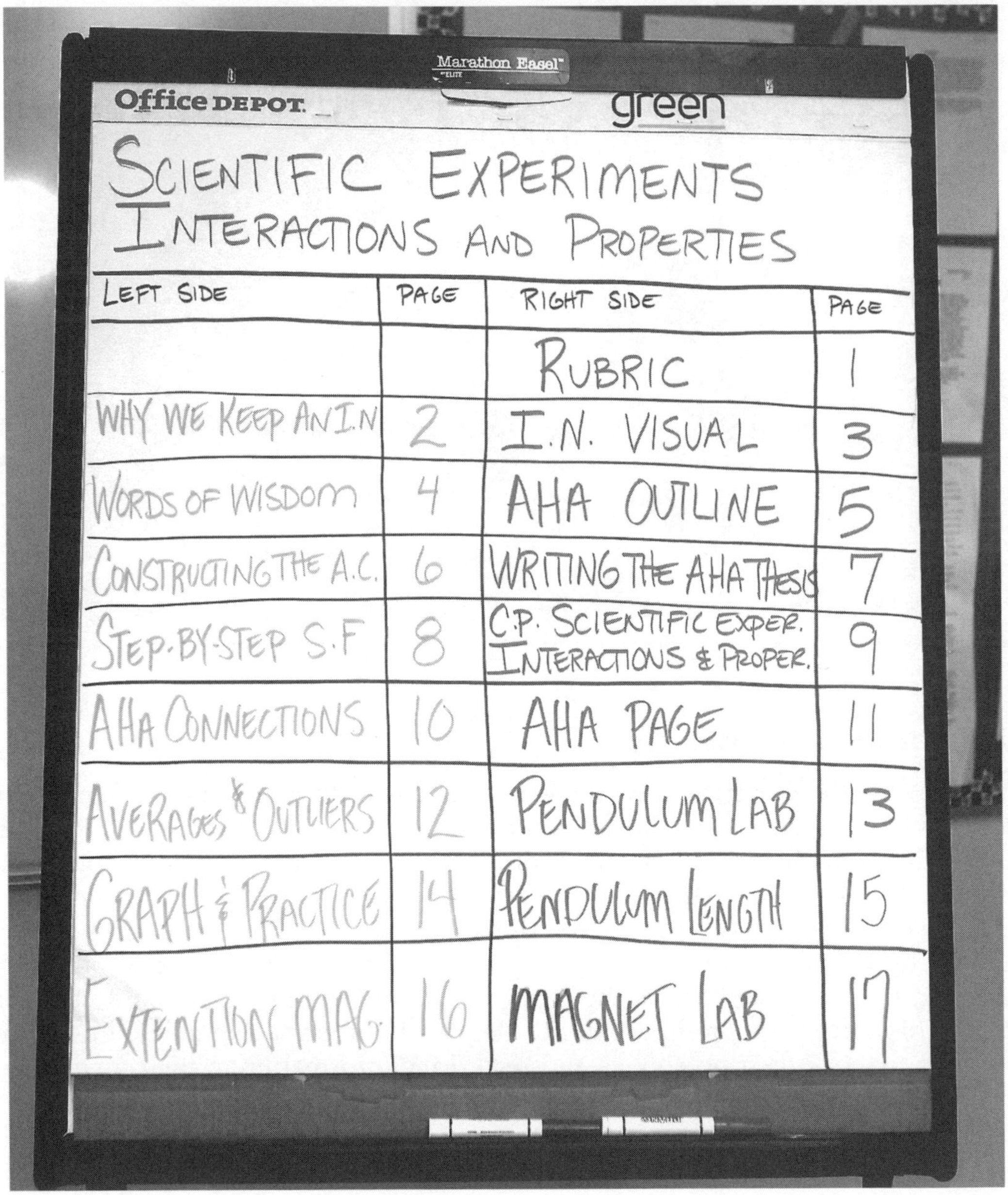

SCIENTIFIC EXPERIMENTS
INTERACTIONS AND PROPERTIES

LEFT SIDE	PAGE	RIGHT SIDE	PAGE
		RUBRIC	1
WHY WE KEEP AN I.N	2	I.N. VISUAL	3
WORDS OF WISDOM	4	AHA OUTLINE	5
CONSTRUCTING THE A.C.	6	WRITING THE AHA THESIS	7
STEP-BY-STEP S.F	8	C.P. SCIENTIFIC EXPER. INTERACTIONS & PROPER.	9
AHA CONNECTIONS	10	AHA PAGE	11
AVERAGES & OUTLIERS	12	PENDULUM LAB	13
GRAPH & PRACTICE	14	PENDULUM LENGTH	15
EXTENTION MAG.	16	MAGNET LAB	17

Day Three Homework

The homework assignment for day three is to create a cover page, on page nine (right side), for the first unit. The rules for a cover page are as follows.

- The student is expected to write the unit title very large on the page, so that it is very easy to read.
- The student must draw a minimum of three pictures that represent the title for the unit. (Share with the students ideas of what they might draw; use pictures from the classroom text to inspire their creativity.)
- The students must color the entire page, corner to corner, using crayons or colored pencils. (They may not use markers on their notebooks.)

The first cover page that students create should be hand drawn (without using computers) to promote student ownership and buy in. Later, cover pages can include computer-generated pictures or pictures from magazines. Figures 3.2 and 3.3 in Chapter 3 show examples of cover pages.

Figure 5.15 An Outline of the First Three Days

Day One	10 minutes	Distribute notebooks, show examples, assign page numbering as homework.
	5 minutes	Label front cover of notebooks.
Day Two	10 minutes	Peer grading of page numbers and class chat about general homework expectations.
	10 minutes	Distribute first eight pages of notebook and discuss homework assignment.
Day Three	10 minutes	Answer student questions about the handouts.
	5–10 minutes	Check homework.
	10 minutes	Demonstrate page titles, labels, the table of contents, and the morning notebook procedure.
	10 minutes	Discuss the cover page homework assignment. **Expect to use the entire day three for setting up the interactive notebook.**

SUMMARY

The first three days familiarize the students with how the interactive notebook is organized and prepares them for an exciting year of science. To guide your students and to create a foundation for quality notebooks, you will want to

- Teach the students how to set up their interactive notebooks step by step through new lessons each day;
- Set the standard for what is going to be expected during the year and keep on track by checking progress daily;
- Model and create criteria with the students; and
- Emphasize neatness.

6

Using the Notebooks

Days Four to Seven

I n Chapter 5, we looked at the first three days of the notebooking process and considered how to construct the notebooks and introduce notebooking to the students. In this chapter, we will look at the next few days of notebooking. While most of the steps in Chapter 5 are completed only once a year (at the beginning of notebooking), many of the steps in this chapter will be repeated each time you introduce a new science unit to the students.

DAY FOUR

Checking Page Nine, the Unit Cover Page

Just as on all the previous days, you will need to check the homework immediately when the students come in to class. Ask students to open their notebooks to the unit cover page. Walk around the room and check each one. You will be surprised at what an amazing job the students have done. As you review the pages, be sure to exclaim over pages well done, and make sure you let each student know you appreciate the effort that was made. Point out different student's cover pages, showing them off to the class with enthusiasm and excitement. Most students are extremely proud of this page. Remember to give each student a grade (full credit, half credit, or no credit) on the student list you have been using each day.

The Trigger Assignment

Today students will complete the first trigger assignment, and the class will formulate the unit question or problem. These processes are explained more fully in Chapter 2, pages 31–35.

Pages 10 and 11

Pages 10 and 11 are the aha connections pages, which you will be constructing together as a class. After students complete the trigger assignment and the class formulates the unit question or problem, students will construct the pages and write the problem statement on them. Page 6, Constructing the Aha Connections Pages, taped in the front of the notebooks as part of yesterday's homework, is a resource for students during this process. (Chapter 2, pages 31–35, has additional information about these pages.)

Day Four Homework Assignment

Day four homework has three parts.

- First, the students need to develop at least three other ideas about alternate unit questions or what they want to know more about. They can be class oriented or personal questions the student wants answered in the upcoming unit. Each question should be written on an individual sticky note, and the student should be ready to share it the next day. This will spur students to think about the unit, about what they are going to learn, and about how it fits into their everyday lives.

- Second, the students need to draw a picture in the center of the two aha connections pages and write the main unit question inside the picture.
- Third, the students need to complete the Interactive Notebook Visual handout on page five of their notebook. Students should place a current picture of themselves over the picture of the student shown on the page. Encourage your students to be creative. They can put their face on a magazine body, create flip pages of themselves making faces, or come up with another idea. I insist that students use a current picture, and if they tell me they don't have one, I offer to take a photo of them using a digital camera. (You might want to do this on day one so that you can print out the photos and supply them in plenty of time for students, giving them no excuses for incomplete work.) Some students want to use baby pictures or pictures of themselves with friends or family members. I discourage such pictures by reminding the students that this is *their* notebook from their present grade level, and the picture in the notebook should reflect this.

> The checking of cover pages as homework should take 5 minutes. The trigger activity should be no longer than 30 minutes. Constructing the aha connections pages and assigning homework should take a combined 10 to 15 minutes of class time, adding up to 45 to 50 minutes of total class time spent on day four.

DAY FIVE

Checking the Homework

As always, when the students come into class, have them open their notebook to their aha connections pages and then flip to the picture that they inserted on page five. Walk around with your class list, and check their work, giving credit for both assignments. Make a big deal over the pictures, and if students will allow you, show several of the pictures to the class. Next, take some time to talk about the different questions that the students generated last night as homework.

After students have discussed the different questions, and maybe posted them in the classroom, have students put them on their trigger page or some other designated spot in their notebook, wherever you choose.

The First Lab Activity

It is now time to complete an actual investigation with the students. In Chapter 2, we discussed the planning process; and in Chapter 3, we looked in detail at how students use the notebooks during investigations. Here are additional insights and tips about using the notebooks during part of the investigation.

- Explain to students that they should leave page 12 blank for now and should be recording their work and their ideas on page 13. Introduce the concept of the right-side page being the input page.

- During the first lab, you will want to model the possible construction of each notebook page. Each page should include visual features that highlight key ideas and findings. You might want to draw pictures, icons, and highlight in your own teacher notebook as you walk the students through this first lab.
- Remind students to include the title and page labels.
- Display a science textbook, and show students the variety of text features that publishers use to focus the reader on a certain idea in the text. Talk about the use of pictures, icons, sketches, highlighted vocabulary words, table of contents, and any other features. This will reinforce features you want students to incorporate when constructing their pages.
- As the students become more comfortable in the upcoming weeks with notebook protocol, they will find their own style and branch out with their own creative ideas. Some students incorporate the use of color coding or keys that correspond to the color use, pictures, or icons they use in their notebooks.
- Obviously, it's the content that counts on each page, so you will need to front-load the above protocol so that it becomes second nature when the students construct each page.

After completing the lab, model how to write the aha connections statement with the class. Include any labels you might want to use, for example, unit number, lab number, line of evidence number, or page number. Some teachers use color or shape to identify the unit or type of "line of evidence." Post the aha connections statement in the classroom as a model for your students, and direct them to write the statement on the aha connections pages.

Figure 6.1   This shows one method for labeling each aha connections statement students write. If the student identifies the unit and page number, it will facilitate reviewing and finding information when it is time to write the aha thesis at the end of the unit.

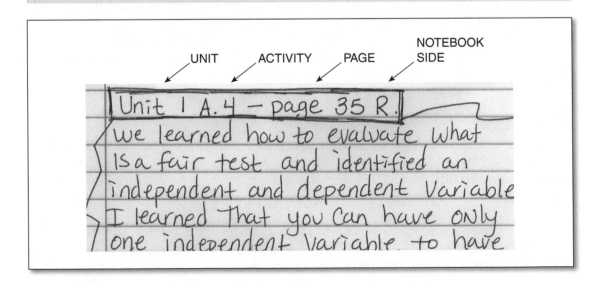

Day Five Homework

Explain to students the idea of the left-side page being the output page, and give a homework assignment for page 12. The homework that is assigned should relate to the lab that was done in class. Assign something fairly simple, something that asks the students to apply what they learned in class to a new situation. Again, this will depend on the lab, but your science curriculum will likely have some suggestions. Most science curricula start off with the use of scientific process skills, so you will likely end up with a focus on procedure, variables, the gathering of accurate evidence, or drawing conclusions from given data.

Using Flip Pages

Because you are giving a homework assignment that goes along with a lab from class, there is no way of telling how much room the students will need to complete the writing that goes on the notebook page. This is the perfect time to go over flip pages with the students. A flip page is exactly what it sounds like. When a student runs out of room on a given page, they get a piece of loose-leaf lined paper and continue the work on that loose piece of paper until they finish. When they are done, they trim the loose leaf page and tape it to the assigned notebook page. They can tape the top of the loose page to the top of the notebook page, or at the bottom; it doesn't really matter. I have even seen students actually tape sideways in their notebooks. Whatever works for them is fine with me. The important thing is that the page is complete and that you can see what is written on the notebook page as well as what is written on the loose page that is taped over it. This will work for peek-a-boo pages as well. The picture that the student draws can go on the loose page taped on top, and the descriptions can be written underneath the flip page that has the drawing on it. It also works for graphs, data tables, handouts, or criteria pages that you want present on the same notebook page. Let us say that you want the students to analyze a graph that you distribute. They can do the work needed, and then tape the actual graph onto that notebook page, as a flip page, for future reference and learning. This helps solve the disconnect that occurs when students have written excellent responses to a question but no longer have the original question. When they look back to make meaning, they have no idea what it all means. Student examples of flip pages are shown in Figures 6.2, 6.3, 6.4, and 6.5.

The homework check of aha connections, questions, and personal pictures will take approximately 10 minutes. The investigation should take about 30 minutes, and writing the aha connections should take about 10 minutes. The total time spent on day five should be approximately 50 minutes.

Figure 6.2   This is an example of a top-taped flip page.

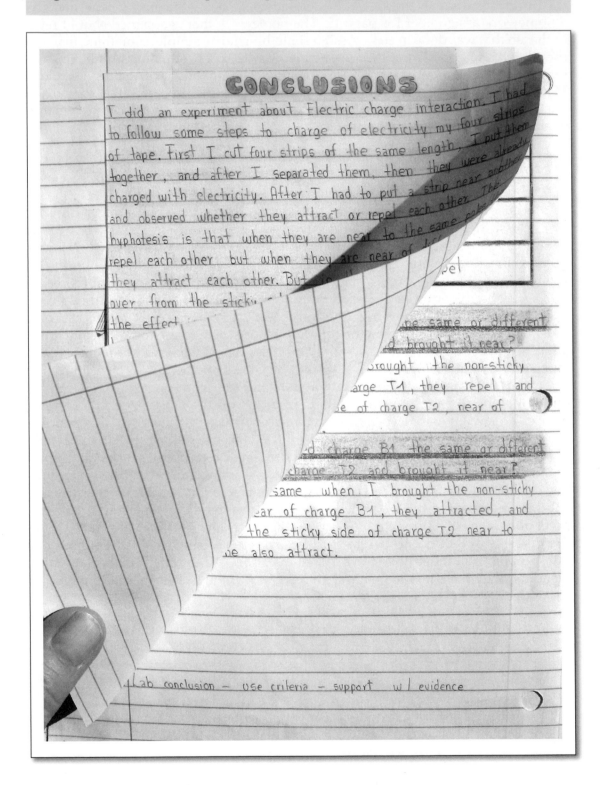

Figure 6.3 This student had a lot to say during a lab activity. He chose to bottom tape for a flip-down page. In fact, this student had more to say and taped on yet another flip page. I have seen bottom flip pages that drop to the floor!

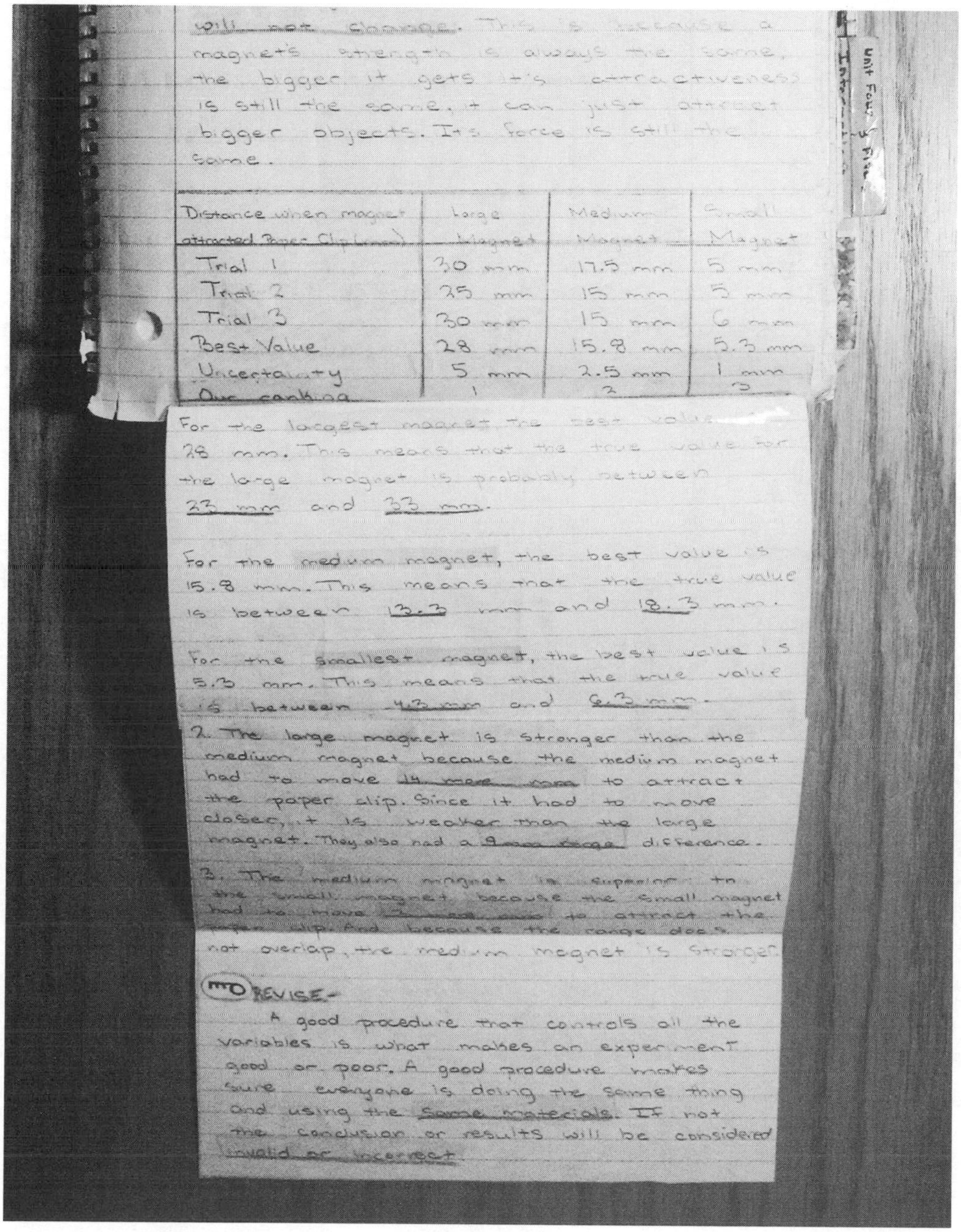

Figure 6.4   This example shows both a side-taped flip page and a bottom-taped flip page. The student used the side-taped flip page to add a picture he found on the Web.

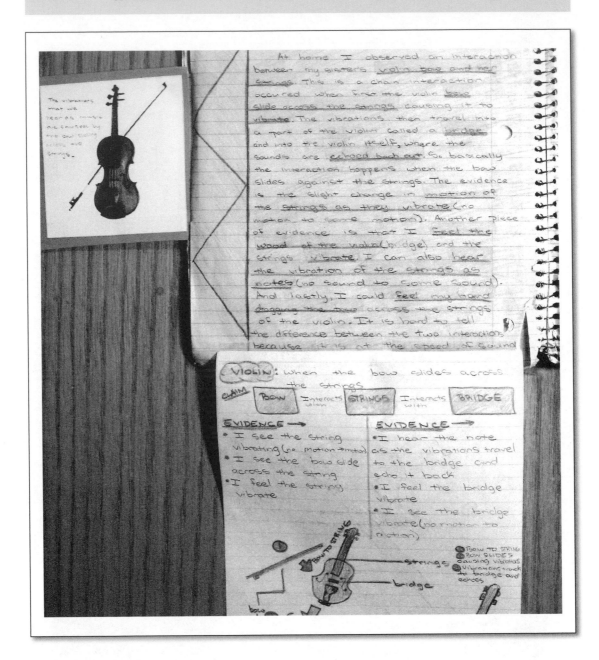

Figure 6.5 This student drew pictures of a type of interaction, and then she described the interaction underneath the picture as a flip page.

DAY SIX

Checking the Homework

Check the homework from the previous day. Look for the utilization of notebook criteria along with the content that was required on that page. Then, show the class some strong examples that were completed by students in the class. Make sure you talk to the class about what makes the samples good. If the first assignment is fairly simple, you will get great work from the students.

Introducing Graphs

Graphing is an essential part of science class and a skill that is continually visited throughout the units all year. Graphs can help the student analyze their data and make meaning of a given problem that they are investigating. For most students, analyzing data and understanding how to read and construct graphs is a challenge. Learning graphing skills takes practice. What better place is there than the interactive science notebook to practice graphing skills? The notebook is a place to refer back to criteria for graphing, to practice graphing, and to learn from prior examples.

Day six is the day of graphs. Whether you ask students to create graphs from scratch or allow students to use Excel or other graphing programs doesn't matter. Students will still need to know what type of graph (line, bar, or pie chart) to use with each set of data. They need to know how to set up a graph using the *x*-axis and the *y*-axis as well as how to label those axes. The students should know how to properly title a graph, and most important, they need to know how to analyze the graph by explaining what the graph shows. I call this part "This Graph Shows . . . ," and this is the conclusion or summary of the student's findings. "This Graph Shows . . ." is an opportunity to tell the reader what they see in the picture (the graph) that represents the data that has been collected. It is an opportunity to talk about trends in the data and to explain the results. This analyzing and making meaning of numbers is the most important part of graphing. The quicker you get students analyzing, the more time you can spend on getting deep into the meaning of why. Then the real inquiry can begin.

Figure 6.6   Graphing is an essential part of the interactive notebook process.

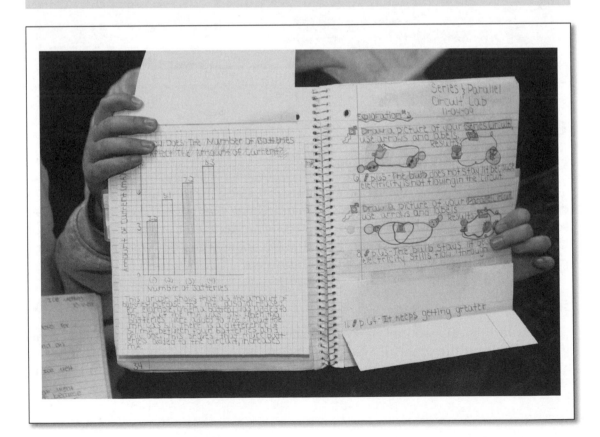

Graphing Criteria

Developing graphing criteria with the class and demonstrating how to incorporate the criteria is an excellent way to introduce the students to your expectations. If possible, I encourage you to work with a math colleague to develop common language for use during graphing and to encourage crosscurricular growth in the students. Students need to understand that graphing in math class is no different than graphing in science class. Using criterion can be a bit rigid at first, but when you are teaching something new to many of the students, it is a great place to start. Eventually there will be variations, but in the beginning, stick to the criteria. When creating graphing criteria with students, I use pictures along with the information to help the visual learners.

Here are elements you might want to include when you are constructing graphing criteria.

For the data table:

- The table should have a title. I typically use "How Does the *Independent Variable* Affect the *Dependant Variable*?" The students can use the same title for their graph because it shows a relationship between the two variables used in the test.
- The table should be constructed like a T chart, in columns and rows. The left side of the chart should represent the independent variable and be labeled accordingly. The right side of the chart should represent the dependant variable and should also be labeled. This is effective because the labels that the students create can also be transferred to the graph when they label the *x*- and *y*-axes.

For the graph:

- The students should be able to choose the correct type of graph to construct.
- They will need to title the graph. The title should represent the relationship between the variables used in the test. (The students can use the title that they created for the table if they use the prompt mentioned above).
- The *x*- and *y*-axis on the graph will need to be labeled properly. (The independent variable should be on the *x*-axis, and the dependant variable should be on the *y*-axis.) I tell my students that the independent variable is the "*I* control, *I* change" variable, and the dependant variable is the "direct response, you have no control, it is what it is" variable.
- The students should know that all data, except outliers, should be used accurately in the graph.
- "This graph shows . . ." or some version of this statement must be present below the graph. The statement should include answers to the tested question. I ask the students to tell me what they see, describe trends, and use the above data to answer the question.

I recommend you keep graphing simple at first. This might seem rigid initially, but once the students become more familiar with graphing, they can increase the level of detail and make their graphs more specific to a given situation where data and circumstances change.

Figure 6.7   Student Example of Graphing Criterion. The graphing criterion should be attached in the notebooks as flip pages for future reference. For homework, the students should be given a set of data to graph on their own so they can practice what you facilitated during class.

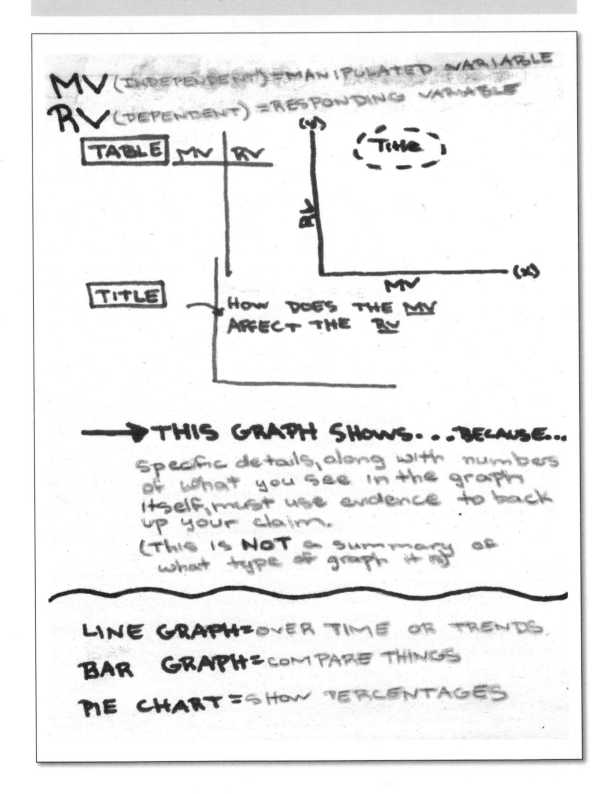

Going over the homework and the lab should take about 10 minutes. Showing some student samples will take another 5 minutes. Creating or going through graphing criteria should take approximately 10 to 15 minutes. The completion of another lab activity that includes the analysis of data should take about 20 minutes, and assigning homework that relates to the classroom lab and graphing will take about 5 minutes. Day six should take approximately 55 minutes.

DAY SEVEN AND FOLLOWING

Checking the Homework

As usual, the first task is to check the student's work to make sure that they have a clear understanding of how to use the graphing criteria. Use examples of student work to show appropriate analysis and to encourage follow through of thought. You might want to show both good and poor examples and walk the students through how to make a poor example better.

Continuing the Process

Continue the rest of your unit with labs, investigations, interviews, research, simulations, and any other lines of evidence. Follow through with the protocol that you set up on the first six days of notebooking. Remember to prethink opportunities for metacognition within the work daily, and model writing frequently through the first 2 months of notebooking, including how to write aha connections statements with the class. Remember to post the aha connections statements in the classroom somewhere and to use arrows to make connections. Periodically, check the student notebooks to see that they are keeping current with their aha connections pages.

At some point near the beginning of the year, students will need to learn how to write summaries and conclusions. How to establish criteria for these is covered in detail in Chapter 7. I recommend that you discuss conclusion and summary writing sometime during the first three weeks of school as part of you regular notebook protocol. This will help ensure student success in writing.

The time line for day seven depends on your lesson plans. It will take 10 minutes to look at the graphs and another 5 to 10 minutes to go over strong and weak student examples. Day seven will include 15 to 20 minutes of notebook protocol time. The rest of the day's activities are up to you. Stick with what you know, and follow the conceptual frameworks for your grade level and state by using the curriculum that you are currently using.

Keys to Effective Implementation

You may feel like you are spending too much time setting up the interactive notebook, but keep in mind that the time you invest now will pay off during the rest of the year. The process is very teacher guided in the beginning because your students are learning the ground rules. Once they understand the expectations and parameters, they will be able to work with much greater independence.

Homework

In the beginning, it doesn't matter much what homework you assign, the important thing is to check it every day. This reinforces the idea that you will be checking student work every day, and it helps them gain a sense of responsibility and follow-through when it comes to homework. At the beginning, spot checks are sufficient; but before too long, you will need to be checking for understanding.

DAY-BY-DAY REVIEW

- Day one is the nitty-gritty of notebooks. You will be working to get students fired up about keeping one.
- Day two is the "let's get real" day, when you establish your expectations.
- Day three is the day of questions, especially about the self-reflection and the aha thesis. Explain to students that you will walk them through the first one and model what to do, so they don't need to worry about this now. Let students know that they will be referring back to these pages during that time.
- Day four is the construction of the aha connections pages, so expect various writing issues. Day four is an opportunity to assess the range and ability of your students when it comes to writing. When you model, ask lots of questions, make the students write the aha connection as you write what they say. This way, you get a feel for how they think and construct a written piece.
- Day five, when students create the cover pages, is the key buy-in day. This will be your first opportunity to praise the students for their work in the notebook. Be positive, but also be honest. If some students fail to meet the expectations, let them know, but also give specific guidance about what they can do to make the cover page better (use color, take your time to be neat, make the title larger, add this type of picture, and so on). Then, offer the opportunity to fix the errors and improve the grade. Day five is also critical because by now you will be able to identify the student who is not keeping up with the class. Call home immediately! Do not wait—you need to nip this problem in the bud and let the other students know that you mean business and that not completing assignments is not an option.
- Day six is the day of graphs, so you may want to solicit help from your math colleagues. Plan ahead of time the criteria you will focus on for your students, and stick to it all year. You can always add to the criteria, but plan on not removing any components from the criteria.
- Day seven and following are when you continue the labs and investigations in the unit. By this time, the routine is established for both you and your students.

Figure 6.8 An Outline of Days Four Through Seven

Day Four	5 minutes	Check homework—page nine, the unit cover page.
	30 minutes	Trigger activity.
	10–15 minutes	Constructing the aha connections pages and assigning homework.
Day Five	10 minutes	Check homework—the aha connections on pages 10 and 11, the questions, and the student photos on page five.
	30 minutes	Lab investigation.
	10 minutes	Writing aha connections statements, assigning homework.
Day Six	15 minutes	Review homework and lab. Show student samples.
	10–15 minutes	Establish and discuss graphing criteria.
	20 minutes	Complete of a lab activity that includes the analysis of data.
	5 minutes	Assign homework that relates to the lab and graphing.
Day Seven	10 minutes	Review graphing homework.
	5–10 minutes	Discuss strong and weak examples of student work.
	25 minutes	Labs, investigations, or other activities according to your unit plans.

SUMMARY

By the end of day seven, your students are familiar with the basics of the interactive notebooking protocol. They know that you will be checking homework everyday, they have started their first unit in the notebook, and they have begun using it during investigations. In addition, students are beginning to see the notebook as a goldmine of information about the expectations for the different assignments they will complete during the year. To continue building the foundation for quality notebooks, it is helpful to remember to

- Check students' homework and progress daily;
- Design homework and in-class activities in which students can extend, reinforce, and make meaning of the concepts on their own;
- Model and create graphing criteria with the students;
- Keep graphs simple at first; and
- Redirect the students to the rubric on page one of their interactive notebook when needed.

7

Learning Through Writing

Writing in science accomplishes several purposes. First and foremost, writing that goes beyond factual comprehension questions and engages students in manipulating content, increases and deepens students' learning (Langer & Applebee, 1987). This is the primary reason for using interactive notebooks in the science classroom. Second, writing is an essential part of the discipline of science—it is what real scientists do and is as essential to the inquiry classroom as it is to the work of real scientists. Third, writing in science helps improve each student's ability to communicate effectively. And finally, writing in science provides a means of assessing student learning—both in terms of ongoing formative assessment as well as a documented progression of student learning.

CHALLENGES IN IMPLEMENTING WRITING

Most students believe that the writing they do in science is minimal. They think all you really do in science is conduct experiments and gather numbers of some kind. Students recognize that you might need to list observations from time to time (of course, these are never in complete sentences), but the idea of writing evidence-supported summaries or thesis papers is simply not what students expect in the science classroom. Getting students to write *at all* in the beginning is, more often than not, quite a struggle. You will hear lots of moans and groans at the beginning of the year; and the truth is, you will still hear moaning at the end of the year. But, students' writing will improve. Your students will be able to express themselves and their ideas in an articulate manner through their writing. The time they spend using writing as a tool to manipulate content knowledge, to integrate content with their personal knowledge, and to construct their own meaning will lead to a deeper understanding of the scientific concepts.

While engaging students in writing stretches both students and the teacher, the fact is that most students are quite capable of expressing themselves orally—in other words, *telling* you what they know. They can talk extensively about how something works or what they see—this is the way they relate to one another in their daily lives. Helping students transfer their observational skills from their out-of-class lives to the science classroom is the goal. By providing practice, you will help students put their words on paper, using their oral-language abilities to inform their written work. The skill of written expression comes with practice and then more practice, eventually becoming a pleasurable habit instead of an overwhelming task.

CROSSCURRICULAR CONNECTIONS

As we work with our students in the science classroom, we can help them develop a more holistic view of the idea that all learning is connected—be it social studies, science, mathematics, reading, or writing. Students need to be reminded that math problems aren't limited to the math classroom, and reading and writing assignments aren't limited to the confines of a language-arts class. While it may be natural to think of these as separate subjects, if we are intentional in our planning we can help students better grasp the concept of crosscurricular connections. Skills and knowledge from various subject areas are essential in every classroom students move to throughout the day. Help your students become accustomed to the idea of crossover. Plan on meeting with teachers of other subjects to establish common vocabulary words that will be used across the curriculum areas. Students will benefit by hearing and learning common terms in all of their classes.

FORMS OF WRITING IN THE INTERACTIVE NOTEBOOK

The following forms of writing are commonly used in science:

- Hypothesis
- Procedures
- Questions
- Results
- Summary statements
- Opinions or reflective writing
- Final conclusions
- Blogs, wikis, or podcasts

In the interactive notebook classroom, we use most of these forms, but we elevate the level of writing and thinking by incorporating two more types of written work:

- Self-reflection papers
- Formal thesis papers (the aha thesis)

MODELING WRITING

Each form of writing (hypothesis, procedure, conclusion, and so on) needs to be modeled by the teacher. By modeling, you show the students how the thinking process translates into written work. When you model each type of writing, include these components—the "think aloud," sentence stems, the use of scientific language, and the criteria you expect students to meet.

Begin the modeling process with pieces of informal writing, and then move to ways to organize writing, and finally, model the formal writing piece. Start the modeling process with students by observing something, taking notes, organizing your ideas, and then generating a formal piece of writing. All these steps are done as a think aloud and are coupled with modeled writing.

As an example, you could observe ant behavior in an ant farm. Place the ant farm in the center of the room and ask students to observe the behavior of the ants along with you. As you observe, think out loud and write your observations in your notebook. (Use an overhead projector or a document camera so that the students can see what you are writing as you talk out loud.) You might say, "The ants seem to be communicating with each other," then *write*, "The ants touch *scape* or antennae to antennae as they pass each other in the tunnel. The ants are lifting sand from one location and transporting it to another location in the farm," and so on. As you are writing, you are expressing your thinking aloud.

After modeling informal writing, you can model how you will organize your observations. You might start with what you know: "I know that the ants created the tunnels because I saw . . . ," and so on. You can do this using a graphic organizer, an outline, or with bullets—whatever format you think will work best for you and your students. You are modeling a way to organize your thinking.

Finally, use the organizational structure you developed to write a summary about ant behavior. Make sure that as you model your thinking aloud, you use the criteria you want students to use and incorporate scientific language and stems. Since you are modeling formal writing, you will need to model the rereading of your written work and demonstrate how you might revise the final summary by adding to it, correcting it, and so on. This signals to your students that you value the reading, revising, and self-correction steps of the writing process.

After completing this modeling process, you could have the students write their own summaries based on the same observation. This will allow the students time to practice and rehearse. Have them work in teams, read each other's work, make suggestions, and then revise the summary.

PROCEDURE WRITING

The modeling process is the same for procedures. When you model procedure writing for students, criteria should include the following.

- Uses numbers or steps
- Lists materials used, with amounts, and how they were used
- Uses clear, specific language
- Mentions how many trials are to be completed
- Identifies the independent and dependant variable
- Identifies how the test was controlled
- The steps should be reproducible; someone outside the class should be able to repeat the process

Some possible stems include

- These events took place in the following order ___.
- In this investigation, first ___ happened, next ___ happened, then ___ happened.
- The materials I used include ___.
- ___ will be measured (observed, timed, weighed) over a period of time. This is the responding variable.
- I will complete this test over a ___ amount of time.
- I will produce ____ (number) samples.
- The manipulated variable is ____, and the responding variable is ____.

SUMMARY AND CONCLUSION WRITING

Although there is amongst teachers an ongoing discussion about the difference between summary and conclusion writing, the consensus seems to be that the summary is written when a scientist is making meaning of data—hence the importance of documenting. The conclusion answers the proposed question with the use of data. In the science classroom, teachers need to be able to see documentation of ongoing thinking processes for purposes of assessment, but they also need to see how analysis and final thinking processes inform the end result—the final concepts learned.

For several years now, I have asked my students to determine the criteria for summary and conclusion writing. The students work as a team to develop the criteria, and then we post the criteria in the classroom and copy it into the interactive notebooks on the appropriate page. Students create examples for themselves to add to the summary and conclusion pages, as flip pages in their notebooks. (See Figure 7.1 for an example of the criteria.) This provides students with a handy reference to the criteria, whether they are at school or at home, as well as a good example of both a summary and conclusion. Students find it helpful to look at good examples of teacher-expected work quality, and since these examples were student generated with teacher support, there is no question as to what is expected.

Figure 7.1   This shows the criteria a class developed for the summary and conclusion pages.

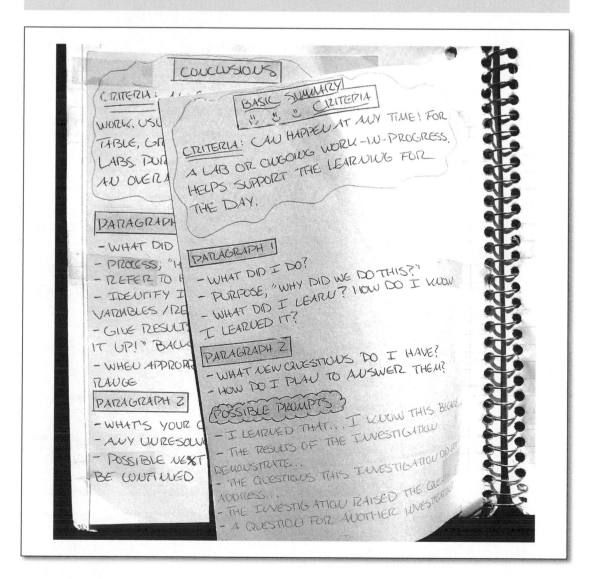

Figure 7.2   Some students use a computer to write their summaries and conclusions. These are then taped into the notebooks.

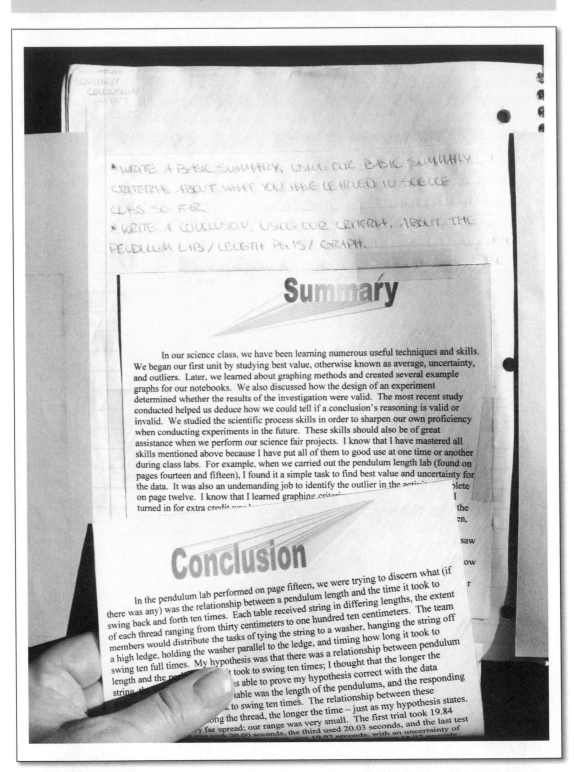

*WRITE A BASIC SUMMARY, USING OUR BASIC SUMMARY CRITERIA, ABOUT WHAT YOU HAVE LEARNED IN SCIENCE CLASS SO FAR.
*WRITE A CONCLUSION, USING OUR CRITERIA, ABOUT THE PENDULUM LAB/LENGTH PG 15/GRAPH.

Summary

In our science class, we have been learning numerous useful techniques and skills. We began our first unit by studying best value, otherwise known as average, uncertainty, and outliers. Later, we learned about graphing methods and created several example graphs for our notebooks. We also discussed how the design of an experiment determined whether the results of the investigation were valid. The most recent study conducted helped us deduce how we could tell if a conclusion's reasoning is valid or invalid. We studied the scientific process skills in order to sharpen our own proficiency when conducting experiments in the future. These skills should also be of great assistance when we perform our science fair projects. I know that I have mastered all skills mentioned above because I have put all of them to good use at one time or another during class labs. For example, when we carried out the pendulum length lab (found on pages fourteen and fifteen), I found it a simple task to find best value and uncertainty for the data. It was also an undemanding job to identify the outlier in the ac̶t̶i̶o̶n̶ ̶c̶o̶m̶plete on page twelve. I know that I learned graphing criter̶i̶a̶ ̶ turned in for extra credit w̶a̶s̶ ̶

Conclusion

In the pendulum lab performed on page fifteen, we were trying to discern what (if there was any) was the relationship between a pendulum length and the time it took to swing back and forth ten times. Each table received string in differing lengths, the extent of each thread ranging from thirty centimeters to one hundred ten centimeters. The team members would distribute the tasks of tying the string to a washer, hanging the string off a high ledge, holding the washer parallel to the ledge, and timing how long it took to swing ten full times. My hypothesis was that there was a relationship between pendulum length and the ̶ it took to swing ten times; I thought that the longer the string, ̶ ̶ ̶ s able to prove my hypothesis correct with the data ̶ ̶ iable was the length of the pendulums, and the responding ̶ ̶ to swing ten times. The relationship between these ̶ ng the thread, the longer the time – just as my hypothesis states. ̶ y far spread; our range was very small. The first trial took 19.84 ̶ ̶ ̶20.00 seconds, the third used 20.03 seconds, and the last test ̶ ̶ 19.97 seconds, with an uncertainty of ̶

Summary Writing

Below, you will find examples of student-generated criteria for the summary.

Criteria for Summary: A summary can be written at any time! It can be written for a lab or an ongoing work-in-progress assignment. A summary helps support the learning for the day. A summary should be divided into two paragraphs and should answer the questions shown below.

Paragraph 1

❖ What did I do?
❖ Purpose: Why did we do this?
❖ What did I learn? How do I know I learned it?

Paragraph 2

❖ What new questions do I have?
❖ How do I plan to answer them?

Possible prompts

❖ I learned that . . . I know this because . . .
❖ The results of the investigation demonstrate . . .
❖ The questions this investigation did not address . . .
❖ The investigation raised the question of . . .
❖ A question for another investigation is . . .

Conclusion Writing

Developing the criteria for writing conclusions is not always easy for students. In the past, some students felt it was important to express their opinion about the results. These students thought it was necessary for the learning process to make meaning of why or at least give their rationale of why. I explained to the students that most scientists believe that opinion has no place in the writing of summaries and conclusions. However, the students countered that these particular summaries and conclusions were written in their personal interactive notebooks. Therefore, opinion was necessary to continue their discovery about a particular concept because it documented what they were thinking. They felt that it would help lead to more discovery and provide opportunity to link back to whether they needed more proof in solving problems. They wanted the opportunity to question themselves and reflect on their own ideas about happenings. I couldn't disagree, so I told the students that if they wanted to voice an opinion, they could do so in a second paragraph in the conclusion as long as they developed criteria for doing so. The criteria below are what the students came up with, and what I used for several years with students.

Criteria for a Conclusion: Conclusion writing is part of the ending process of overall work. It usually is placed after a data table, graph, or sometimes multiple explorations. The purpose is to make meaning of an overall concept or idea. A conclusion should be divided into two paragraphs and should answer the questions and satisfy the conditions shown below.

Paragraph 1

❖ What did I do?
❖ Process: How did I do it?
❖ Refer to hypothesis
❖ Identify independent and dependent variables and their relationship to each other
❖ Give results
❖ State your claim, and back it up with *all* data
❖ When appropriate, use uncertainty and range
❖ Discuss possible outliers

Paragraph 2

❖ What is your opinion about the results?
❖ Why do you think the results were so?
❖ Any unresolved questions?
❖ Possible next step if the investigation is to be continued

Possible prompts

❖ The basic procedure was . . .
❖ When I changed_____, _____ happened.
❖ This graph shows . . .
❖ I believe . . . because . . .
❖ I wonder why _____ happened.
❖ I would like to try . . . because . . .
❖ I predict . . . would happen if I do . . .

The first year I invited the students to generate the criteria for summary and conclusion writing was a powerful learning experience for me. Students felt empowered by the opportunity to choose the criteria and eagerly bought into the idea of writing. The sense of ownership of their notebooks was very high. The idea that giving students more choice would have a positive impact was not new to me, but I had never really experienced it or seen it play out quite like this. The following year, I decided to use the same criteria, telling my new students that the previous year's students had written them. The sense of empowerment and ownership wasn't the same. So now, I recreate the organic experience every year with each incoming group of students. I ask several leading questions and allow the students to do the rest. The criteria stay pretty much the same from year to year, with small changes here and there, but the students feel the buy in because it is organic for them. I have to rewrite the criteria on poster paper each year, but this is a small price to pay to ensure high levels of student ownership!

WRITING A SELF-REFLECTION

The interactive notebook classroom goes a step further than traditional science instruction by incorporating two major pieces of writing into each unit—the self-reflection paper and the formal paper called the aha thesis. The purpose of the self-reflection paper is to allow students an opportunity to reflect on their own learning and show their in-depth understanding of the work they are doing. They write about what the specific unit means to them and how they see themselves as a learner in the classroom. This assignment provides a place for students to express their unique thoughts and be honest with their opinions. It is also promotes awareness of the impact they have on others and their contribution as a group member. Finally, this paper encourages students to think about how they can improve their learning and their final grade in the class.

The self-reflection papers are assigned at the end of each unit throughout the year, so students usually complete four to five of them in a year. The handout with step-by-step directions about how to generate the self-reflection paper is taped inside the front of their notebooks, so it is always available. After completing a unit, the students tape their completed self-reflection paper onto a notebook page at the end of the unit. Figure 7.3 shows the handout. Figures 7.4 through 7.6 show one student's self-reflection paper.

WRITING A THESIS PAPER

The final assignment during a unit is the formal paper called the aha thesis, which deepens and solidifies the student's learning during the unit. In Chapter 2, we discussed the Aha Connections pages and the idea that the work students do on these pages informs their aha thesis paper. To review, each unit is focused on a central question or problem. Throughout the unit, students will conduct investigations planned to provide them with evidence they might use to answer the question. These lines of evidence, which are gathered from investigations, research, experts, and so on, are used to write the formal aha thesis paper.

Working as individuals or in teams, students take all of the lines of evidence that they have collected and compile them into a multiparagraph essay with an introductory paragraph, body paragraphs that summarize each line of evidence, and a closing paragraph. Students can use the lines of evidence as stems for writing their aha thesis. Figure 7.7 is the handout students use as a guide when writing their aha thesis. Figure 7.9 is a sample of an aha thesis paper. This may be given to students so they have a good example of the paper.

When writing an aha thesis, students will have to organize their evidence in a logical order. Most students create an outline page in their notebook, which specifies the exact information they plan to use in their thesis. Figure 7.8 is an outline page from a student notebook.

The students then write the formal essay, based on evidence. During this assignment, students will be practicing critical thinking, using evidence to back up a claim, citing sources, and using written communication, including paraphrasing.

Figure 7.3   This handout walks students through the construction of the self-reflection paper. Step 2 asks students to choose which pages in their interactive notebook best support their Aha moment. This provides the student with a focus for evaluation. Later in Step 4, the students are asked to rate their work by using the rubric on page 1 of their interactive notebook. This gives the students an opportunity for self-evaluation. If they can identify the problem, they can fix it, and move forward in their work.

How to Write a Self-Reflection

You will be expected to write a reflective essay at the end of each unit that shows your in-depth understanding about the work you are doing. Be honest and open in sharing your thoughts and opinions.

Step 1: Count the number of the assignments we have completed for this unit, and record it at the top of your reflection.

Step 2: Choose four pages from this unit that best supported the Big Aha in your unit thesis, two from the left side and two from the right side, and list them on your reflection below the assignment count.

Step 3: You will now be writing three paragraphs.

   Paragraph 1: Write specific reasons for why you chose the four assignments that you listed.

   Paragraph 2: Explain why these pages best support your unit thesis. Give specific examples.

   Paragraph 3: What do these assignments reflect about your skills as a student? For example, you may write that they show that I am organized, I am good at analyzing, I was very thorough, creative, my information was very accurate, I made connections from one assignment to another, and so on. Make sure that you cite specific examples from the pages you listed.

Step 4: This will be Paragraph 4. In this paragraph, you will rate your own notebook. Use the rubric to rate your work as a 10, 9, 8, 7, 6, or 5. How do you think your notebook measures up and why? Use specifics from the rubric, and relate it directly to the pages you listed. (Use examples.)

Step 5: This will be Paragraph 5, the last paragraph of your reflection. Hurray! Answer the following questions:

   • What information did you learn that was new to you? Give specific examples.
   • How did your notebook help you in this unit? Again, be specific.
   • How could you improve your notebook? Please explain.

Please type your final draft, and tape it as a flip page in your interactive notebook as specified by your teacher.

Figure 7.4   Example of Self-Reflection Paper. This figure shows how students complete Steps 1 and 2, identifying how many assignments were completed in a unit and which assignments represent their best work. For Step 3, in the first paragraph, this student explains why she chose these four assignments. She is clear about her reasons: she worked very hard on these assignments and can see the improvement in her own work. Recognizing their own improvement is important for students as it enhances the self-corrective phase in learning.

Self-Reflection

15 assignments completed in Unit One, Cycles 1-3

Pages chosen to reflect on:

- o   14; Graph and Practice, U1C1A2
- o   15; Pendulum Length Lab, U1C1A2
- o   23; Evidence of Interactions, U1C2A1
- o   44; Calculating Density and Mass and Volume, U1C3A5

I feel that the pages chosen above are good examples of some of my best work. I spent countless hours – yes, hours – on page fourteen, perfecting my graphs and making sure my skills were sharp enough to meet the expectations of all of us in the eighth grade. It also shows how much effort I put into my work, not just because of the content, but also because I spent much time perfecting the appearance of the work. On page fifteen, I tried my very hardest to honestly answer the questions, test everything properly, and conclude the experiment properly. It was a huge effort, like lifting a pile of bricks, but I finally got there in the end. I am proud of these pages, considering they were created soon after I entered eighth grade. On page 23, I also spent much effort on perfecting the written material and the outward appearance. I was very concentrated on how professional my work appeared and how advanced the material was. This page was completed nearer the beginning of the year than now; again, I am proud that I accomplished so much when I was just beginning the year. The most recently completed page, 44, demonstrates how I've improved. My level of thinking has risen since I completed science fair, and I no longer feel like a seventh grader. It is easier for me to grasp a concept now, and I can analyze data much better than before. All these pages are my pride; I spent a great deal of time working on each of these, and I feel that this effort has paid off.

I chose these four assignments because they are well done and well support the main points in my big idea thesis. I had discussed in great detail how we concentrate

Figure 7.5   The student continues completing Step 3. In the second section of highlighted text she explains that she chose this assignment because it answers the second key question of the unit. This also supports the aha connections. To complete Step 3, Paragraph 3, she cites specific examples from the chosen work that show her good analysis skills. She took an opportunity to give her opinion about what was happening in the lab, and used accurate data in her analysis. In the last paragraph she rates her notebook, which is Step 4. In my experience, most students are more critical of themselves than the teacher would ever be.

very much on the scientific process and how it is our greatest tool in science. Graphing is a key portion of the scientific process; it gives us a visual picture of our data and therefore makes it easier to analyze. The explanation of the graph is also very important in data analysis; it forms a basis for our results paper written soon after graphs are completed. The next page, Pendulum Length Lab, is just as vital to the scientific process as Graph and Practice. We began with a question to solve, and hypothesized what the results of the test would be. Then, we collected data and summarized what our results were. After finishing the graphing on the previous page, we wrote a conclusion for the lab. After this page, I chose page 23, discussing interactions. Our second key question for Unit One was what an interaction was. This lab provided us with an opportunity to break down any interaction; we wrote, step by step, exactly what happened in the interaction. It was essential for us to learn what an interaction was, and this lab helped us answer that question. The final page was one on density. Here, we learned what properties are (part of the third question of the unit) and we were discussing how properties allowed us to determine the composition of an object. Density is an important property, more important than other attributes like color or texture. It allows us to determine what material an object is made of, perfectly answering our key question. These are the reasons for my choosing of such pages in my notebook to reflect on.

Each of these assignments reflects certain skills I have as a student. On page fourteen, I demonstrated that my analyzing skills are pretty well developed, because this page was completed just as I came back from summer vacation filled with nothing but playing video games and reading novels. On page fifteen, I feel I was fairly thorough in my explanations and was very clear when expressing my opinion. On page 23, I was very thorough as well, describing the interactions as much as possible. I think my information on the page was very accurate as well, because I explained so much about each interaction. Finally, on page 44, I demonstrated that my calculations are accurate; I am very strong in math, and I think I showed that very well on this page. I was very brief, but I think I conveyed my opinions clearly in the summary found on this page.

I would probably rate my notebook an eight or nine, though it would be closer to a nine. I definitely understand the concepts, and occasionally I do think outside the box. My notebook does have all components required, and I spend my time organizing each

Figure 7.6   As she continues completing Step 4, this student is very specific about what needs to be done to improve her work; for example, she writes, "I can go more in depth." In the last paragraph, she completes Step 5. She cites specific concepts and exact page numbers as examples of her new learning. She reports that the notebook helped her organize her thoughts, visualize her progression, and improve her study skills. In answer to the final question, "How can you improve your notebook?" she writes that she needed to take more time and refrain from procrastination.

page and confirming that it is at least decent quality. I use diagrams occasionally and I color as much as possible. <u>All I feel that I lack is that I do not always give my work my best effort. There are days that I am very sluggish, and I do not express my opinion well enough or go beyond the barrier that I've broken so many times. On page 49, for example, my summary is very concise and shows that I have an understanding of the concepts we learn in class, but I could have added more. I can go more in-depth than what I had written on that day.</u> This is my problem on most days; I am a little too concise occasionally, and I sometimes reach the point of vagueness.

I learned so much in this unit. It has been a turning point in my life, because I never realized that I actually have more potential than I always thought. I feel like I thought of myself underrated before, but after this unit, I know I can do anything. It was like my mind was being compressed, and that compressor has finally been released. <u>I fully understand the scientific process and can employ it anywhere (pages fourteen and fifteen). I realize that thousands of interactions occur each second, and I can describe each of these in the greatest detail (page 23). Finally, I have learned the different properties of objects and how to utilize them to discover more about certain materials (page 44).</u> My notebook allowed me to organize my thoughts; I took all my thoughts and threw them down on paper, like Harry Potter and the Pensieve. I look back and see how much I have progressed, and I set my shoulders to embrace what is to come next. The best way to improve my notebook is to improve my study skills. I do not procrastinate as much as I used to before middle school, but I still lose concentration occasionally. To not idle anymore. . .this would be the best way for me to improve my notebook. I lose sleep sometimes because I have wasted too much time. <u>This the best way for me to improve my notebook, to stop procrastinating, because I will have sharper concentration and therefore also have more time to ponder the world of science.</u>

Figure 7.7   This handout explains exactly how the aha thesis is formulated. Use your modeling protocol the first time you require students to write a thesis, and, if possible, show a student sample from the previous year.

How to Write an Aha Connections Thesis

What is an aha connections thesis?

It is a thesis paper, generated by you, that addresses the Big Aha or big problem of the unit, using evidence gathered along the way.

1. Let's get started by gathering what you need.

- Go back to the aha connections pages in your interactive notebook.
- Look for the key ideas or concepts you identified from the unit.
- Which lines of evidence best support these key ideas?
- You are now going to use these lines of evidence in your thesis to support your key points.

2. Now, begin by writing your introductory paragraph.

Introductory paragraph:

State the purpose of the unit and the key ideas and concepts learned.

(Hint: That's what you just identified in the four bullets above.)

3. Now you are ready to write the body of your thesis.

Body paragraphs of the thesis (usually three to five paragraphs):

In each of the following paragraphs, give details on one of the key ideas chosen from above.

Use your lines of evidence from your aha connections pages to support your thinking.

(Hint: There is no need to reinvent the wheel; use your own words from the aha connections pages in your interactive notebook.)

4. You are almost there—time to wrap it up.

Final paragraph—conclusion:

- Restate your purpose from the thesis statement.
- Give your thesis the "Hollywood" wrap up.
- Leave a final impression on the reader.

Figure 7.8 Most students create an outline before writing their aha thesis paper. This shows how one student used headings to organize his outline.

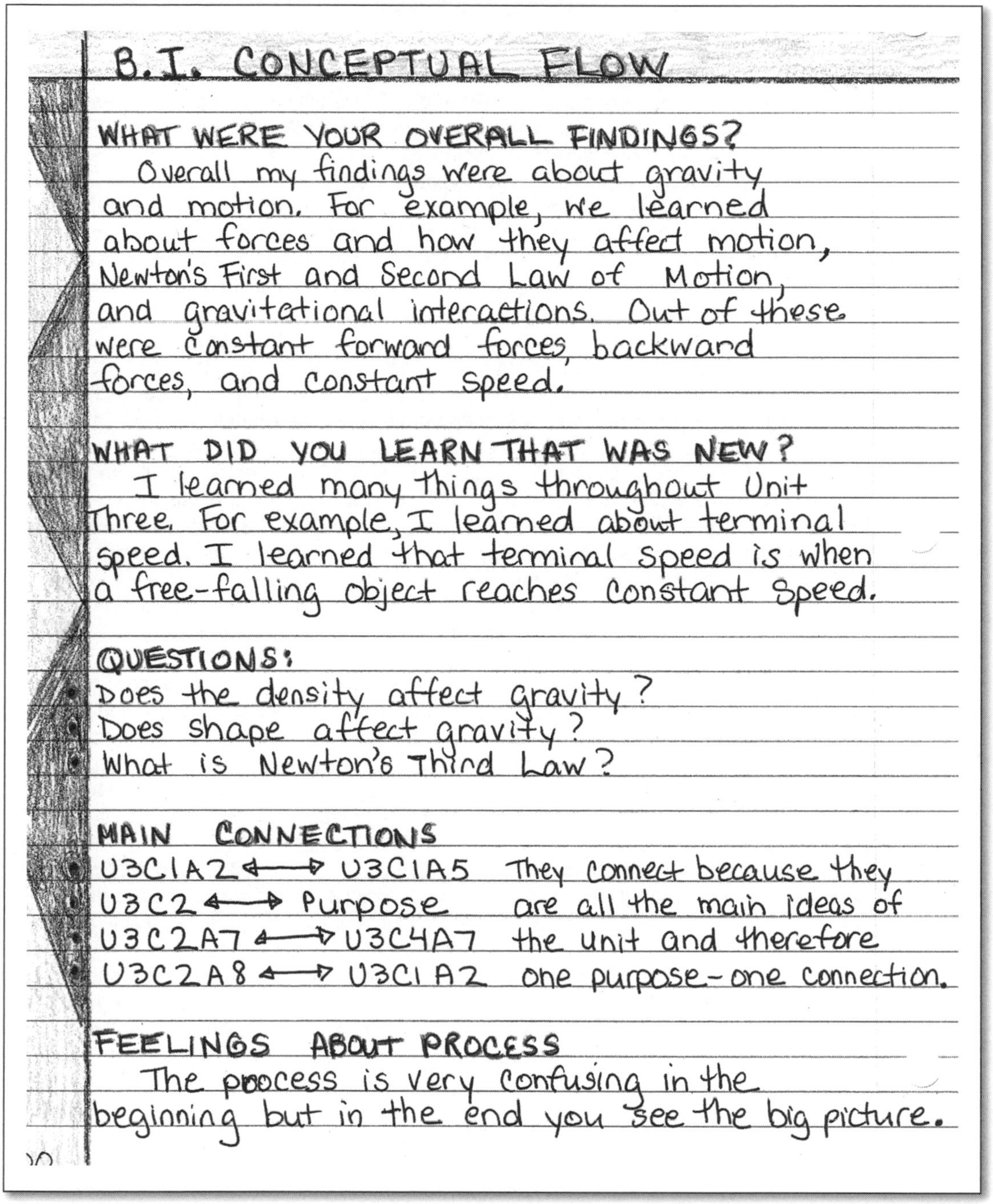

B.I. CONCEPTUAL FLOW

WHAT WERE YOUR OVERALL FINDINGS?
Overall my findings were about gravity and motion. For example, we learned about forces and how they affect motion, Newton's First and Second Law of Motion, and gravitational interactions. Out of these were constant forward forces, backward forces, and constant speed.

WHAT DID YOU LEARN THAT WAS NEW?
I learned many things throughout Unit Three. For example, I learned about terminal speed. I learned that terminal speed is when a free-falling object reaches constant speed.

QUESTIONS:
Does the density affect gravity?
Does shape affect gravity?
What is Newton's Third Law?

MAIN CONNECTIONS
U3C1A2 ←→ U3C1A5   They connect because they
U3C2 ←→ Purpose   are all the main ideas of
U3C2A7 ←→ U3C4A7   the unit and therefore
U3C2A8 ←→ U3C1A2   one purpose - one connection.

FEELINGS ABOUT PROCESS
The process is very confusing in the beginning but in the end you see the big picture.

Figure 7.9 Sample of Aha Thesis for Use With Students

Unit 2 Aha Thesis

We learned many important concepts throughout Unit 2. In this unit, we learned how scientists identify different interactions in terms of energy. We also learned how to calculate the speed of objects, where motion energy comes from, where it goes, and why it changes. Exploration of these concepts builds a foundation that will allow us to have background experience as we continue to delve into the world of psychics and science.

In this unit, we discovered how scientists identify interactions and how they describe them in terms of energy. In the "Energy Description Lab," we learned that interactions can be identified by the different characteristics. We also discovered that scientists describe interactions in terms of energy by using energy diagrams. Energy diagrams include the type of interaction, the energy source, an energy transfer arrow, the energy receiver, and evidence. In the "Energy Changes Lab," we learned that energy is never created or destroyed but is constantly changing or being transferred. This can be represented in energy diagrams by bubbles that connect to the source and receiver. Energy diagrams are graphic organizers that illustrate the transfer of energy from the energy source (such as a person's foot) to the energy receiver (such as a soccer ball).

We continued to expand on this topic and incorporated new information in "The Fabulous Wake-up Machine." We learned about the different and specific types of energy that go with certain interactions. For example, electrical energy is transferred in an electric-circuit interaction, light energy in a light interaction, and mechanical energy in a mechanical or mechanical-wave interaction. We then incorporated these specific types of energy into the energy arrows in our diagrams. In addition, we created chain-energy diagrams to show how each element in our Fabulous Wake-Up Machine affected different systems and our senses.

In this unit, we also discovered how to describe the motion of objects with constant and changing speeds. In the "Constant Speed" investigation, the class learned that objects that have constant motion are neither speeding up nor slowing down.

The speed of an object is equal to the distance traveled divided by the time elapsed. Another method that can be used to calculate the speed of an object in constant motion is to calculate the slope (rise/run) of the line when it is graphed. If two quantities are plotted on a coordinate grid and produce a straight line, they have a linear relationship.

In the "Changing Speed Lab," we learned that the average speed of an object with changing speeds can be determined using the same mathematical formula, distance divided by time. We also learned that when two quantities are plotted against each other and the resulting line is not straight, there is a nonlinear relationship between the quantities. The speed of an object will only tell how fast it is moving, not the direction of its motion. *Velocity* is a term that is used to describe how fast an object is moving and the direction it is moving in. For example, if a bicyclist is moving nine miles an hour east and six miles an hour west, the cyclist's velocity is nine miles an hour east and six miles an hour west. We found that scientists use the term *acceleration* to describe how quickly an object's velocity changes. An object has acceleration when its speed changes (if it speeds up or slows down), when it changes direction (turning or moving in a circular path), or both.

In Unit 2, we learned that motion energy is the energy that an object has because of its motion and that it is constantly changing. As a class, we came to the conclusion that as the speed of an object increases, its motion energy increases. As the speed of an object decreases, its motion energy decreases.

In the "Motion Energy Chart" investigation, we learned that there are four different types of mechanical interactions: applied, friction, elastic, and drag. An applied interaction is when two rigid objects push or pull on each other. A friction interaction occurs when two surfaces rub against each other. A drag interaction takes place when an object moves through a gas or liquid and its motion is resisted by these elements. An elastic interaction occurs when two objects push or pull on each other, and at least one of them is stretchy.

We continued to expand on this topic in the "Energy Changes" investigation. We learned that the energy source in an interaction always decreases in some sort of energy and is transferred to the receiver, which always increases in energy. For example, when someone is the energy source in applied interactions, they generally decrease in stored chemical energy while the receiver increases in motion energy. In friction interactions, the source generally decreases in motion energy while the receiver increases in thermal energy (heat). In drag interactions, the source generally decreases in motion energy, and the receiver increases in motion energy. In the "Elastic Interaction," we discovered that elastic objects increase in stored elastic energy when they are stretched or compressed. When the elastic object is released and it returns to its original form, the stored elastic energy is changed to other types of energy, such as motion energy. For example, in an elastic interaction in which a tennis ball is the source and the racquet and ball are the receivers, the source decreases in motion energy while the receivers increase in stored elastic energy. In the situation in which the racquet is the source and the ball is the receiver, the racquet decreases in motion energy, and the ball increases in motion energy because the stored elastic energy is changed into motion energy.

Comprehension of these concepts is vital in our learning of physics and science. In this unit, we learned about how scientists identify different interactions in terms of energy. We also learned about speed, motion energy, specific types of energy, and how they change in the four different types of mechanical interactions. Each activity that the class did helped us gather key ideas about these concepts. The information that we obtained through labs and investigations will help us in future units and in our journey through science.

ASSESSMENT

Interactive notebooks provide the teacher with the opportunity to assess student learning all of the time. The written work students complete in the notebooks can be reviewed both formally and informally to better understand the extent of student learning. The interactive notebook is also a very useful self-assessment tool. The notebook rubric helps students understand the teacher's expectations, and students can use it to assess their work throughout the year. The rubric specifies the expectations for the pages in the notebook and guides students in organizing their work. The various writing activities in the notebook give students the opportunity to reflect and make meaning of the lesson. As they complete writing assignments and use evidence they gathered to explain or state their case on a topic, they will become more aware of what they know and what they don't know.

Assessing the notebooks can be time consuming and requires careful time management, particularly since timely feedback is necessary to help students keep progressing in their work. Rather than trying to assess every individual piece of writing students complete, you may want to focus on one specific piece of evidence from the writing to assess student understanding. This might be a summary or conclusion at the end of an investigation, a chart or graphic organizer, a revised key question, or another piece of writing. You could focus on content understanding or process skills. Or, you may wish to focus on the areas you know are problematic for students.

The Notebook Rubric

The notebook rubric shown in Chapter 5 (Figure 5.4) has been modified and developed over several years as I reviewed student work and reflected on which elements of notebooking contributed to students' understanding and which did not. Even so, nothing in the rubric is sacred, and I encourage you to modify it to meet your own needs. You may also wish to create rubrics to assess the work that students do on a daily basis. Daily rubrics could be developed by adapting the notebook rubric to change the focus and some of the language. Key points to remember about formal assessments are that they need to be standards based, should help students clearly understand what is expected, and should be easily accessible to all students.

Research shows that assessments improve student learning, so use high-quality assessments that are well developed and thought out. When designing rubrics, think about your purpose and whether or not the rubric will help you meet it. Ask yourself the following questions:

- Is the rubric clear?
- Is the work sample you are collecting the appropriate method to use for the context?
- Does the rubric specify that students provide the evidence you need to assess their mastery of content knowledge?
- What specifically will the students say, write, or do to show you that they have understanding of the concept?

Formative Assessment

Formal assessments can tell you whether a student has mastered a concept, but they don't tell you what that student needs to do to master it. In addition, they don't always allow you to see how errors in thinking led to an incorrect answer or how close the student is to understanding the concept. Formative assessment, on the other hand, is an effective classroom practice that can improve student understanding. In their landmark review of research findings, Black and Wiliam (1998) found that the use of formative assessment gave all students significant learning advantages. In addition, several studies they examined showed that low achievers had the *largest* gains. According to Heritage (in press), "Formative assessment is a process that takes place continuously during the course of teaching and learning to provide teachers and students with feedback to close the gap between current learning and desired goals."

Guidelines for formative assessment are found in *Classroom Assessment and the National Science Education Standards* (National Research Council, 2001). According to these guidelines, formative assessment should help students better understand

- Where they are trying to go (in terms of their conceptual understanding);
- Where they are currently; and
- How they can get from where they are to where they want to go.

Working with students to answer these questions, both by giving them feedback and by helping them reflect upon their own progress, is the essence of formative assessment. Teachers can use conversations and notebook comments to help students move forward with their learning.

Interactive notebooks will help you see a progression in the students' learning, provide the evidence you need to determine whether the below-basic students are making gains and meeting the grade-level standards, and provide opportunity for your students to self-assess and become active in the grading process.

Guidelines for Effective Assessment

When you give feedback, make sure that it is timely, useful, and appropriate. Giving feedback as soon as possible is more effective for your students and can also influence the next learning sequence. To help increase the usefulness of your feedback, reinforce the criteria you previously established, reviewing exactly what you were looking for if necessary. Identify what was learned well, and describe what needs to be learned better. Go beyond discussing whether something is right or wrong, and give your students guidance on how to improve their learning or their work.

Remember to use questions to probe students' thinking and assess their understanding. Avoid looking only for a particular answer and thereby cutting students off or stifling them during the learning process when their responses aren't what you expected. Students need opportunities to reflect on their own thought processes.

Keep in mind the end goal: increased student learning. When an exploration is complete and data has been collected, end with a whole-class, evidence-driven discussion to help students internalize scientific thinking and models of talk. Frequently during these discussions, opinions change, and students gain an opportunity to revise ideas and conclusions. To encourage this kind of revision on an assignment, students can be rewarded with extra points for revising or adding to their original thinking.

Remember that formative assessment is a valuable source of information for improving your instruction, indicating what worked in your lesson, what needs improvement, and what you might need to do in the next lesson. When assessing student work, record or document what you see, and look for patterns or trends in the student learning to help guide you. Then ask yourself questions such as these:

- Is this a background-knowledge issue or a new-content-knowledge issue?
- If I change that question a little, would my students demonstrate a better understanding?
- Are my students all making the same mistakes?
- Are the mistakes due to errors students made during the process, such as the recording of data or faulty equipment?
- Or, are there issues with communication—do students lack the writing or language skills to express themselves correctly?

After answering these questions, you will be in a better position to make the appropriate adjustments, modifying teaching and learning activities to meet the needs of your students.

Work with another colleague to practice using formative feedback. Learning to give good feedback takes practice, and when you practice with other teachers who are like minded, you are sure to get great results.

Assessing Student Writing

Make sure that you identify for yourself what you want the students to know as they walk out the door each day. This guides what you will be looking for in the writing. Ultimately, evidence of conceptual and content understanding should be present in the student writing. The notebooks should include a progression in the student writing, reflective work that is self-corrective, and a clear thinking process that you can follow easily. You should see the following kinds of writing and thinking:

- Identification of similarities, differences, and comparisons
- Identification of patterns or ranges as students analyze data and statements such as, "My data shows a range from . . . to . . ." or, "The patterns I noticed were . . ."
- Connections to observations that students made in class during investigations
- Evidence of students applying their knowledge and relating it to the content
- The use of scientific language
- The use of specific lines of evidence and information
- Statements such as, "The relationship between . . . and . . . are important because . . . ," "Because this happened, I predict that . . . will happen," "My evidence confirms . . . because . . . ," and, "My results confirm . . . that . . . had no effect on . . ."

Use rubrics to identify key words and concepts that you will be looking for in the student work. For example, some writing should include qualitative statements, such as, *I heard . . . , the color is . . . , I felt . . . ,* or *I smell . . . , the shape changed from . . . to . . . ,* and so on. Other writing should include quantitative statements such as, *the distance traveled was . . . , the temperature was . . . , the average height was . . . , the data collected showed . . . ,* and so on. Show the class examples of excellent student work along with work that needs improvement, and together analyze the differences between the work samples to help students see how they can improve.

As you assess student writing, be careful to read what students are actually writing, rather than just looking for a large amount of content. Remember to give specific feedback about how students can progress. As the work improves, the need for feedback increases.

Avoid writing directly in a student's interactive notebook, particularly if you use a pen. Red pen is especially negative and should not be used. Give feedback orally or on sticky notes. Remember, the idea is to allow the student to revise or add to their thinking in the notebook. In my experience, writing directly on student's notebook pages causes them to feel stifled and decreases the likelihood that the student will revise the work. However, if you use sticky notes on pages as needed, students can take your advice to improve their existing work, and then remove your note. Their sense of ownership of the notebook is intact. In my classroom, students who want additional credit for a revised page leave the sticky note with my advice on the page, show their revised work, and then remove the sticky note after I have given additional credit. The end result is that students are encouraged to revise their thinking and feel comfortable doing so because each notebook is viewed as a work in progress rather than a final product.

SUMMARY

Writing in science is an integral part of the learning process and is a tool to foster and develop each student's thinking. Interactive notebooks incorporate several different kinds of writing assignments to increase students' content learning. Assessment is used to make decisions about where to go next and to improve instructional practices. Both formal and formative assessments can empower teachers and students. When formative assessment is practiced properly, and feedback is given in a timely manner, student learning increases. Formal assessments provide students with a meaningful opportunity to synthesize their learning. Use these tips for implementation:

- Model the thinking and writing for your students. Be sure to use sentence stems and the specific desired criteria as you model the process. Modeling seems contrived at first, but it will become more natural with practice.
- Think aloud about what you want to communicate. This modeling will help students see the kind of thought processes they need to engage in.
- Be explicit with your students about your expectations, building rubrics together. Share both strong and weak examples of student work with the students, reviewing the qualities that make one piece a good example and another piece a poor example.
- Provide students with opportunities for feedback. Allow time in class for students to read each other's work and provide feedback to classmates.

8

Learning Through Discussion

M eaningful discussion in the science classroom allows students to express their ideas, hear and build on the ideas of other students, and reconsider and revise their own ideas. All of these processes promote student learning. Student-driven discourse that moves learning forward, also known as *accountable talk*, brings the development of ideas into the public arena—the classroom community—and provides opportunities for students to build their understanding of essential ideas by learning from one another. Students can talk about their ideas, learn from each other, and come to consensus based on their common experiences during an investigation. These discussions also give the teacher the opportunity to assess learning and identify students' misconceptions.

Of course, you could implement the use of notebooks without accountable talk just as you could incorporate accountable talk without notebooks. However, in the science classroom, using the two together promotes powerful learning. Notebooks serve as a rich resource for the data, ideas, and information students need for in-depth classroom conversations and discussions. Conversely, accountable-talk conversations enhance the work students do in their notebooks. The interplay between the work students do in the notebooks and the work they do during their conversations is cyclical; each feeds and builds off the other.

How can accountable-talk sessions improve the quality of the work students do in their notebooks? During these sessions, students are forming and reforming their understanding of concepts. Students can take their new understandings and add them to work in the notebook or use them to revise existing entries. Students emulate the work of real scientists by engaging in focused, "professional" discussions, and then they take what they learned in those discussions and add their new learning to the written record in their notebooks.

Accountable talk serves another important purpose—it provides an arena where students can use scientific language. We know students need the opportunity to use new vocabulary properly and in context in order to retain and reuse the language in new situations. While the teacher can introduce new terms and post them on the wall, unless students practice talking and using the new language, their working vocabulary will not expand. Student conversations and discussions provide an appropriate place for students to practice the use of key terms as the teacher promotes the use of scientific language during each accountable-talk session.

FEATURES OF ACCOUNTABLE TALK

Accountable talk includes specific features: accountability to the learning community, accountability to knowledge, and accountability to standards of reasoning. Accountability to the learning community means listening to one another, building on other's ideas, disagreeing respectfully, and being committed to group learning. Accountability to knowledge means using specific, accurate information and asking questions about claims. Finally, accountability to standards of reasoning means linking claims and evidence and building arguments carefully and clearly (Michaels, O'Connor, & Resnick, 2008). These features are an ideal match for the kind of work we want students to do using their interactive notebooks.

Notebooks facilitate accountable-talk sessions by providing an at-hand resource packed with data and information from investigations. As students are talking and thinking, they draw from concrete examples in their notebooks. When students are asked, "What is your evidence for that claim?" the notebook provides the evidence that supports their ideas. All notebooks have a uniform table of contents and common page numbers, allowing all students to easily follow along and add to the discussion based on their own personal evidence, which may be used to either support or refute the ideas being discussed. As all work is recorded in the interactive notebook, students are also able to draw connections from previous investigations, allowing them to use all relevant data rather than only selective pieces. Scientists follow this practice, and students must learn how to do so as well in order to draw valid conclusions.

INTRODUCING ACCOUNTABLE TALK

Students need to be taught how to talk accountably, just as they need to be taught how to use their interactive notebooks. Modeling, practice, and designated amounts of time are key to making accountable talk a regular part of the science classroom. The first crucial task is to create a classroom environment where students feel safe enough to share their thinking. While disagreements are expected during accountable talk, classroom norms can be established to help ensure a safe environment that breeds good thinking and the building of ideas. Just as scientists solve problems by working together, our students need to learn to do the same. This can take many forms: discussions in pairs, discussions in small groups, and discussions as a whole class to organize and synthesize ideas collectively.

The more you involve students in creating a positive environment, the greater their buy in will be. Ask your students to brainstorm how scientists find out what other scientists are working on or researching. Students may come up with such ideas as reading books or articles, reading Web posts, e-mailing, and, hopefully, discussing their work. Ask your students more about *how* they think scientists discuss. What kinds of words might they use in their discussions? How might they start a sentence? If two scientists disagree, but need to work together to reach a solution, how might their conversations sound? Move from the discussion about scientists to the development of a class list of norms for accountable talk. Help students identify such features as active listening, giving people equal time to share, providing opportunities to ask questions, responding to questions asked, and using evidence (from their notebooks) to back up their claims. Chart students' ideas, label them Classroom Norms for Accountable Talk, and post them on the wall.

For the first accountable-talk session, direct students to pair off. Ask them to face one another, notebook in hand, and look directly at their partner. Give them a prompt to discuss that is simple and that all students can connect with, for example, "Explain the creation of your unit cover page." Direct students to

- Actively listen to their partner (remain in eye contact, nod when they understand, and don't interrupt or ask questions until the partner is finished);
- Share air space (both partners get an equal opportunity to talk);
- Bring their notebooks and use them during the conversation (notebooks provide your evidence);
- Ask your partner at least one question, and respond to their answer; and
- Never use put-downs (stupid, dumb idea, what were you thinking? and so on).

Remind students that these ideas are on the class-created norms chart, and that they can refer to the chart during the activity as necessary. This activity should take approximately three to four minutes to complete, and it allows an opportunity for students to practice speaking, listening, and positioning. (You may wish to use a timer for this activity to monitor the time.) This first activity is done in pairs because pairs are the most comfortable speaking zone for students (as opposed to speaking in front of a group) and are also the easiest type of accountable talk for the teacher to manage. This strategy is called "Turn and Talk."

The idea is now established that there are norms for scientific discussions. These norms are the same ones that will be used during all future accountable-talk sessions.

Figure 8.1 Students find Turn and Talk awkward at first but they quickly become accustomed to sharing their ideas and learning with a partner.

STRATEGIES FOR ACCOUNTABLE TALK

Although you have developed norms with the students, they won't yet truly know how to conduct these types of discussions—even with their natural tendency to talk. You will need to use a variety of other modeling techniques and strategies to support students and build their capacity for meaningful discussions.

Using Sentence Stems

One way to support students is to introduce the use of stems. When students feel stuck or are unsure of how to express themselves, they can rely on these stems to maintain focus in the conversation. Displaying the stems where students can easily access them during a conversation is encouraging to students. You can write the stems on chart paper and place the chart in a prominent spot in your classroom, include them in the interactive notebook, or place lists of the stems in protective sleeves and display them at each table in the classroom.

Expressing Your Opinion or Thought

I believe . . .

I think . . .

In my opinion . . .

I'd like to make a connection to . . .

I'd like to interpret . . .

I can make an inference (or, I infer) . . .

According to my prior knowledge . . .

I predict that . . .

Responding to a Classmate's Thought

I agree with . . .

I agree with . . . , but I would like to add . . .

I partially agree with . . . , but I believe . . .

I partially agree with . . . , but I would like to add . . .

I disagree with . . .

I understand that you are saying . . . , but . . .

I'd like to build onto . . .

I'd like to include . . .

I'd like to justify my thought . . .

I'd like to respond to . . .

I can assist . . .

I just had a thought: What if . . . , or maybe . . .

I was wondering . . . What do you think?

Asking for Clarification

I need clarification on . . .

I need assistance with . . .

Could you repeat that please?

I'd like to hear what you are saying, could you please speak up?

Could you justify that please?

I have a question . . .

So, in other words, you think that . . .

Could you please give me an example of that?

You made a claim that . . . ; could you back that up?

Students may feel strange when they begin to use sentence stems and the conversation may seem contrived. This is a valid feeling, but with continuous use, using stems will become more natural. Remind your students that scientific discussions include scientific language, and that talking about ideas in science class *should* feel different from having a personal conversation with close friends on the schoolyard. Along with norms, the use of these stems should be constant during accountable-talk sessions in class.

TALKING TASKS

Once norms have been established and stems have been introduced, you will need to provide the opportunity for students to talk. These sessions should be driven by questions you pose about the work students are doing. Simply providing an opportunity to talk will not be enough to get the ball rolling for most kids: You will need to provide strategies to get them talking. What typically happens is a student will say, "Oh, I think this . . ." And other students will simply respond with, "Yes, I agree with you." This brief conversation ends without any probing or deep thinking. Giving students small tasks to drive the conversation in the beginning will help.

The Interview

In this strategy, students in groups of three or four read a passage or article and ask prepared questions of each other in order to make meaning of what they read. They interview each other and present to another group their collective findings.

Card Sort

Provide a group of students with a set of cards that need to be sorted by category. Give each student in the group a few of the cards, and instruct the students to work as a group in order to categorize all of the cards. Ask the students to describe the characteristics of each category. What do the items in each group have in common, or how is each group different from the other groups? To push student thinking further, you could ask students to reorganize the cards according to different categories. Or, you could ask students to come up with an overarching concept for the cards, and share their ideas with another group.

Interpreting Visuals

Promote conversation by giving a map, graph, or picture to your students, and ask them to interpret it. The students in each group should come to consensus on the meaning of the visual and, if appropriate, discuss other questions, such as why the scientist chose to represent his findings in this way.

Tape Talk

Another effective strategy to use after your students are comfortable with one another is recording each group's conversation. After making the recordings, have groups exchange tapes and then have each group listen to the tape and present the other group's findings. Use question cards to keep the groups focused on solving the problem and presenting the ideas to the class.

These are just a few strategies to help you get started and create that safe environment that students need in order to have meaningful discussions. The process can be slow going at first, but once students get the idea, this becomes their favorite part of the lesson. Most students love to talk, and this fits right in with their natural tendency to do so. Remember to encourage the use of scientific language and the use of a good up-to-date notebook. They both lead to super conversations.

Figure 8.2   Providing a variety of activities for small-group discussions helps ensure student interest and engagement.

WHOLE-CLASS DISCUSSIONS

The most difficult type of accountable-talk session to manage is the whole-class consensus discussion. You need to listen carefully to facilitate and guide the discussion and to provide opportunities for all students to participate.

Facilitating Conversation

When facilitating the conversation, the teacher poses questions only when needed to push the students' thinking further or to gently guide the students in a particular direction. For most educators, this technique can be difficult because teachers love to talk, get to the point, and move on. Instead, the goal is to become a gentle guide, someone who uses questions to steer the boat as it floats. You will need to practice asking meaningful questions at just the right time, without interjecting approval-type statements. Stay away from statements such as "That's right," "Excellent answer," or "Great, so let's move on to. . . ." Provide the appropriate wait time, and encourage all types of opinions, from those on target to those that are off base. The conversation should appear to have no leader, but be just a group of people engaged in a group discussion.

A meaningful discussion can go completely off topic very quickly, so even though your leadership should be subtle, you will need to use questions to gently guide the discussion back to the main focus. Try to allow the group to come to its own conclusion. At the end of the discussion, ask a student to summarize the overall outcome, keeping your own opinion out of it. Not only can this be hard for the teacher, it will also be challenging for some of your mastery-minded students. They crave the correct answer as well as approval from the teacher and will ask questions like, "So, is that right?" or, "What do you think?" You can respond to questions or comments by saying something such as, "Does the evidence show . . . (whatever they came up with)? Then, trust what you already know the answer to be." "The class came up with . . . , so it must be what you think is right" or, "Is there really a right or wrong answer here?" Answering a question with another question is thought provoking. Remind your students that science is the search for understanding and that is what we practice in class. In time, they will become accustomed to this approach to teaching.

Facilitating Participation

So, how do you get all students engaged and participating in the group discussion? Start by positioning. Ask the students to gather in a common meeting place, in close proximity to each other, where everyone can see and hear one another. You can call it the "Fireside Chat," "Coming to the Pit," "Circle Time," or some other term that is meaningful for you. Remind students to speak up, look at others when they address the group, or look at a specific person when addressing that person. One of the most important rules is that students should not look at you when they are addressing the group. They will do this out of habit, watching your body language and looking for approval from you. (This practice has been ingrained in students from the first day of kindergarten.) Break them of this habit by sitting slightly outside the circle, and every time they look at you, point to the group until they shift their head position toward their classmates. You will need to do this a lot in the beginning; but with time and practice, students will get the point.

Make sure that all students are inside the circle with their bodies in discussion position, not slouching or turning away. (This is the same position as the one used during Turn and Talk.) Check that all students have their interactive notebooks present on their laps and ready to use. Although it may be hard to believe, the notebook provides safety and comfort for most students, just like a security blanket. When the students are in position and the conversation is flowing, listen for the "frequent flyers." If these students begin to dominate the conversation, interject timely questions, such as, "Paul, what do you think about what Stacy said?" or, "Paul, what do you think Stacy means?" Address comments to those students who have been quiet but who look engaged. Try not to embarrass students or catch them off guard, as this will backfire. Remember, you want to encourage students to talk. You could also choose students to speak using common tactics, such as writing student names on craft sticks or rolling dice. These methods will keep students engaged in the conversation and ready to respond because they know they may be asked for their opinion at any moment.

One gentle strategy is to ask a student to find evidence to back up another student's opinion and to chime in as soon as he finds something that supports or refutes it. This allows the conversation to continue, and the student is not under pressure to speak immediately. When he does speak, he will be offering evidence rather than opinion.

You may have some students who initially find it difficult to form their own opinion. If, after a few group consensus discussions, you notice that particular students never participate, take them aside later, and ask what they think of what their peers were saying. Then, encourage them to share their ideas with the group next time. Or, during a conference session, you might mention to a student that she has good ideas in her notebook, and you would like to see her participate more in the whole-group discussions because you think that other students would benefit from her strong ideas.

Whole class accountable-talk discussions can be a lot like learning how to catch a wave. It can be tough to judge the wave at first. If you take off too soon, you end up under the wave in a swirl of surf. If you take off too late, you miss the wave entirely. Knowing exactly when to take off allows you to ride the wave in to shore, but you can only learn this with practice. So practice, practice, practice, and eventually you will be able to ride the wave during class discussions.

EFFECTIVE QUESTIONS AND DISCUSSION

We've explored the importance of discussions as part of the learning process for students. Questions promote thinking, encourage talking, and initiate learning. However, when time is short, teachers have a tendency to cut the questions and limit the discussions. When we do this, students have no time to synthesize, they leave the room with misconceptions, and now you have to build on shaky ground with tomorrow's new concepts. In my experience, cutting short the time for discussion isn't worth it. Better options would be to shorten the explore portion of a unit a little to allow for discussion; or split the lab into two days, so you have the time to follow through. It is important for students to share their ideas, to make meaning, and reflect on the learning. Questions help center the students on what is important in the lesson and target the focus concept.

Figure 8.3   Students constantly refer to their notebooks during the class discussion.

When you ask students questions, remember to wait for a response. The school environment forces us to watch the clock closely, so that we feel rushed; and in turn, we rush our students. In order to keep myself from such behavior, I have learned to nod my head with great frequency. I do so while uttering such phrases as, "Interesting," "How do you know that?" or "What is your evidence?" When students ask for answers, I commonly reply with, "I don't know, what do you think?" Students just love that! Being a good listener is equally important. When you really listen, you can actually hear the student, and you can respond with more follow-up questions—questions that engage the students at the table in a deep conversation long after you have left.

THE "ACCOUNTABLE TALK" CLASSROOM

As students become more proficient at accountable-talk sessions, you will hear all students talking and engaged in conversation with minimal prompting by you. During whole-class sessions, participation will shift from just a few students dominating the conversation to a lively interchange between numerous students. You will hear deeper discussions between students for longer periods of time. Students will be building on each other's ideas and will use data to back up their ideas rather than offering unsubstantiated opinions. The use of scientific language should increase, and you should hear students using this language properly. Since students are more comfortable sharing their ideas, the noise level in your classroom may increase, and you may need to set a timer to bring student conversations to an end. While you will need to be careful to give students enough time to thoroughly express and develop their ideas, once students become comfortable, they will never seem to have enough time. Since you cannot devote the entire class to accountable-talk sessions, using the timer seems to be a happy compromise.

SUMMARY

Collaborating with others to expand understanding of scientific concepts allows students to develop a number of important 21st-century skills, which will enhance student learning in any subject. Accountable talk brings the development of ideas into the public arena and engages students in coming to consensus about those ideas. Students draw from the data and information in their interactive notebooks to fuel these discussions. The work students do during accountable-talk sessions reinforces and strengthens the work they do in interactive notebooks. The opposite is also true—the work students do in interactive notebooks reinforces and strengthens the work they do during accountable-talk sessions.

To achieve these benefits in the classroom, teachers need to

- Give opportunity for students to practice talking like scientists;
- Provide prompts in order to get the ball rolling;
- Nurture a safe environment for students; and
- Use whole-class discussions to reach a scientific consensus.

9

Conclusion

I nteractive notebooks are an effective tool to open up new horizons of learning that students will need in the 21st century. They have enriched my teaching and improved student achievement and communication. The following list reviews the many powerful benefits of using interactive notebooks.

STUDENT BENEFITS

High Levels of Buy In

My students think they are just having fun, writing, coloring, exploring, collecting data, researching, graphing. They have no idea that these strategies will lead to increased achievement. This relates directly to student buy in. If you give them structure with purpose, the students will love science, love their notebooks, will be proud of their work, and will work with you even on the days when the work is not so fun.

Internalized Learning

When an exploration is complete and data has been collected, ending with a whole-class discussion where the conversation is evidence driven, students internalize scientific thinking and models of accountable talk. Most of the time, opinions change, and students gain an opportunity to revise ideas and conclusions.

Thoughtful Writing

Students' writing and thinking improves. They write specifics about science processes, and they extend their ideas to their own lives. Their summaries and conclusions are more logical and results based because they are relying on self-generated data. Figures 9.1 and 9.2 show how one student's thinking (expressed in his writing) progresses.

Organization

As the weeks and months pass by, the students become noticeably more organized in both thinking and work habits. Their mind maps are more complete, more useful, and the teacher is able to clearly see their thinking processes, as visible in Figures 9.3 through 9.5.

Self-Assessment

The interactive notebook is a valuable self-assessment tool. The students understand the teachers' expectations and use the notebook rubric to assess their work throughout the year. When students write or graph evidence-based findings, they get a chance to assess what they know.

Self-Reflection

The writing and discussion activities built in to this approach give students the opportunity to reflect and make meaning of the lessons. They can use the evidence they gather to explain or state their case on a topic. They can reflect on the new ideas introduced and make connections to ideas and concepts that they learned earlier in the year.

Figure 9.1   This is a good example from a student at the beginning of the year. He refers to his conclusion as a class conclusion, so he must have written it after the whole-class discussion, which is fine. I hope to see his personal ideas written down first, with corrections, on later pages throughout the year. He uses evidence to back his claim, but he doesn't go into detail about the results or ask any questions after the completion of the lab.

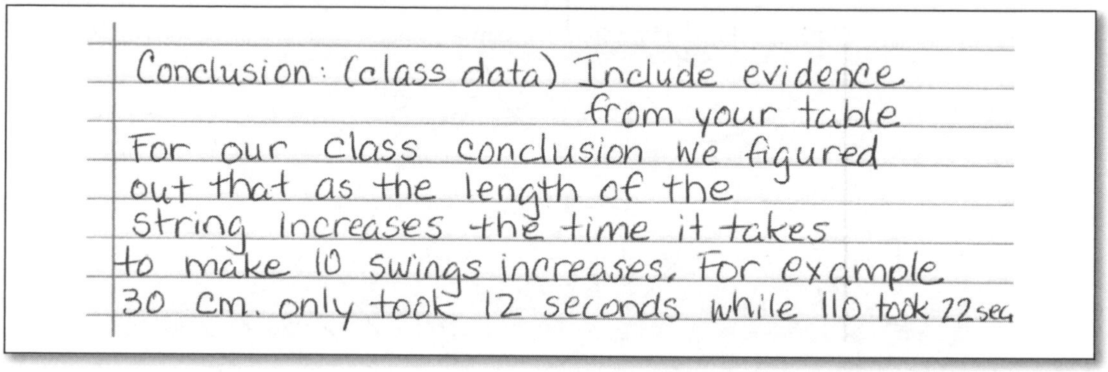

Conclusion: (class data) Include evidence from your table
For our class conclusion we figured out that as the length of the string increases the time it takes to make 10 swings increases. For example 30 cm. only took 12 seconds while 110 took 22 sec.

Figure 9.2   This is the same student one month later. Notice the brief description of procedure and reference to the data table on the next page. (I would hope to see specific references in writing in later months.) The student self-corrects along the way, asks questions, and makes note of a possible extension activity to continue his exploration of gasses. Clearly there has been a progression in his writing from the previous sample (Figure 9.1).

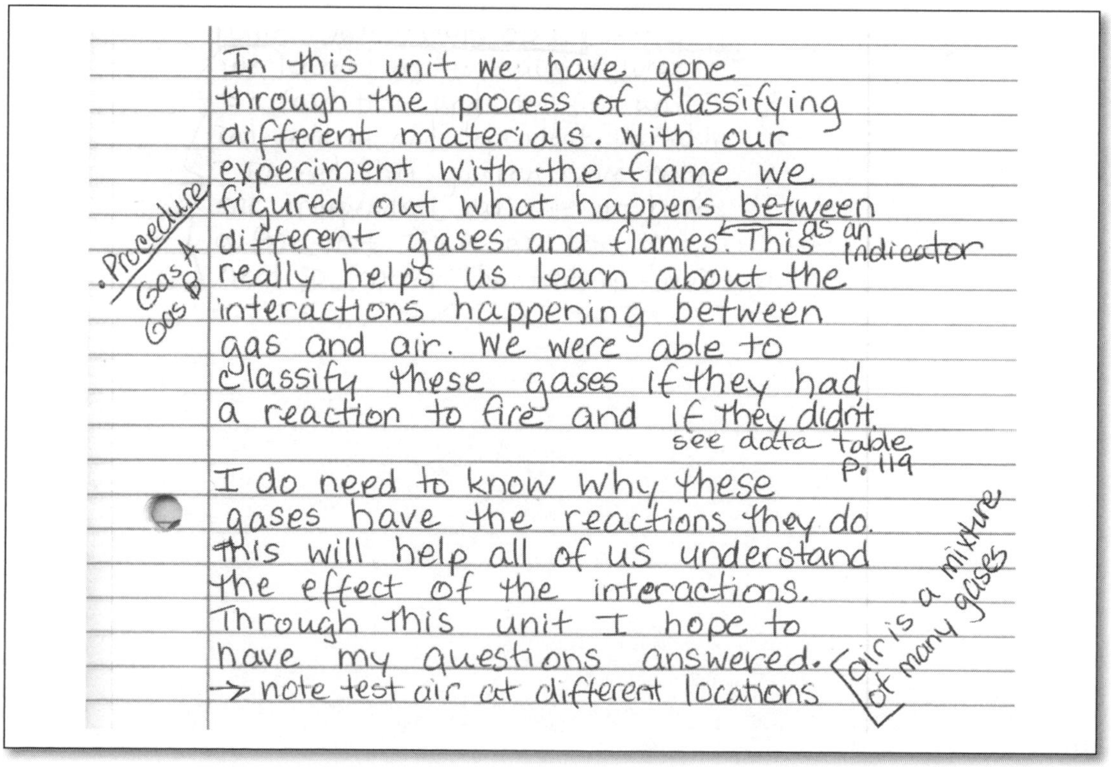

In this unit we have gone through the process of classifying different materials. With our experiment with the flame we figured out what happens between different gases and flames. This as an indicator really helps us learn about the interactions happening between gas and air. We were able to classify these gases if they had a reaction to fire and if they didn't. see data table p. 119

Procedure Gas A Gas B

I do need to know why these gases have the reactions they do. This will help all of us understand the effect of the interactions. Through this unit I hope to have my questions answered. air is a mixture of many gases
→ note test air at different locations

Figure 9.3 This is a graphic organizer done by a student at the beginning of the year. Very little of his thinking is displayed on the page.

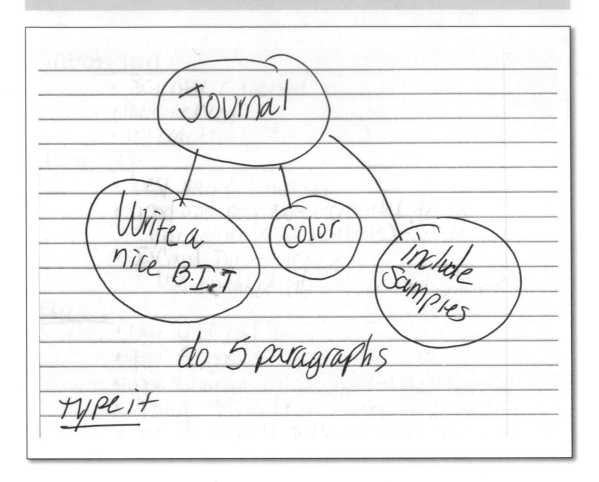

Figure 9.4 One month later, the same student is bulleting his ideas for each paragraph, showing the teacher some of his thinking.

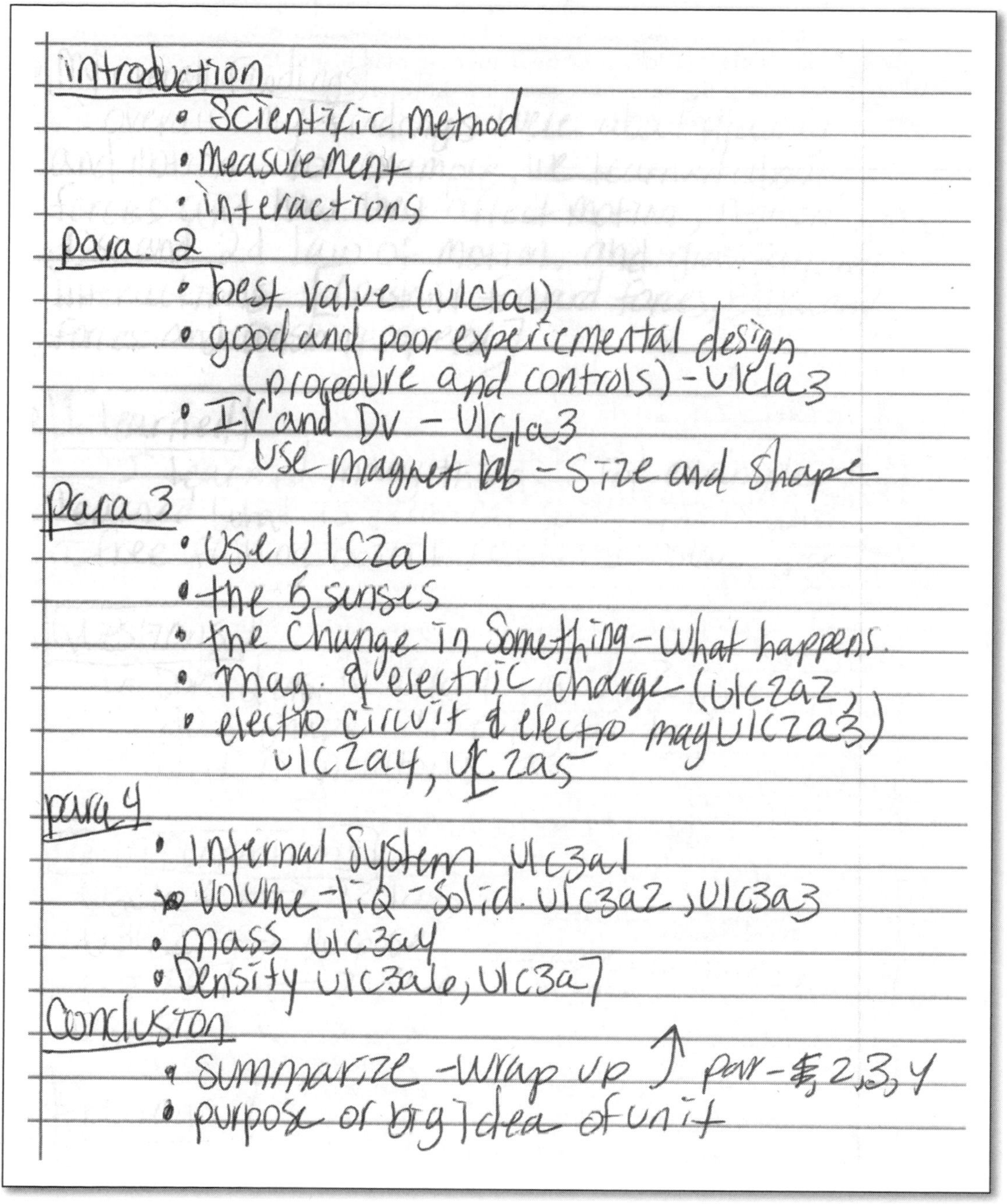

Introduction
- Scientific method
- measurement
- interactions

Para. 2
- best value (U1c1a1)
- good and poor experimental design (procedure and controls) - U1c1a3
- IV and DV - U1c1a3
  Use magnet lab - size and shape

Para 3
- Use U1c2a1
- the 5 senses
- the change in Something - what happens.
- Mag. & electric charge (U1c2a2,)
- electro circuit & electro may U1c2a3)
  U1c2a4, U1c2a5

para 4
- Internal System U1c3a1
- Volume - liq - solid. U1c3a2, U1c3a3
- mass U1c3a4
- Density U1c3a6, U1c3a7

Conclusion
- Summarize - wrap up ↑ par - #,2,3,4
- purpose or big idea of unit

Figure 9.5 Two months later, the same student is organizing his writing in concepts. He uses complete sentences, includes questions and evidence, and even includes a personal opinion, at the bottom of the page, about his process throughout the unit. Again, there is an obvious progression of his thinking and the organization of his thoughts for his written thesis. He makes giant strides from September to March, and the teacher can clearly see where the student is going and how he is getting there.

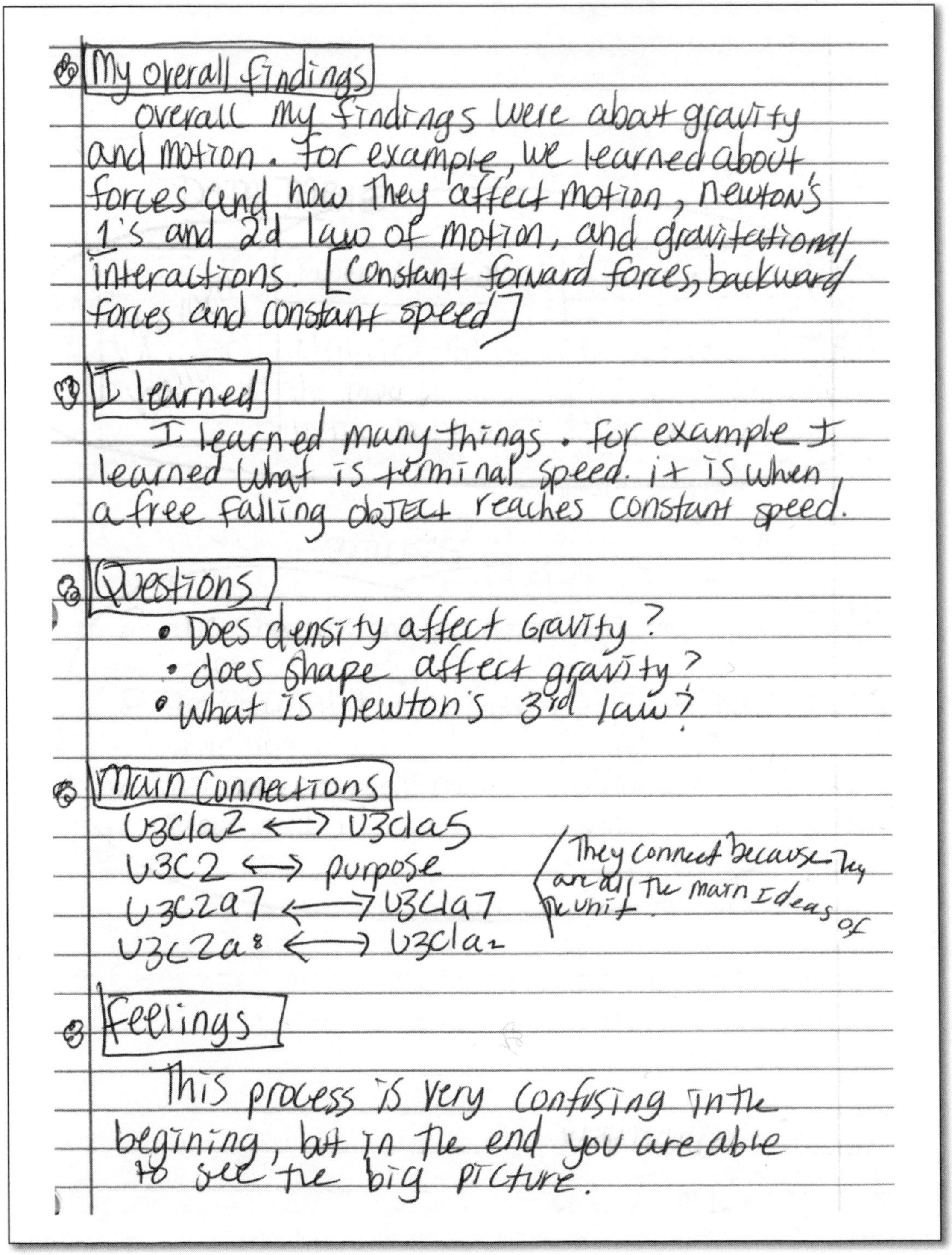

My overall findings
overall my findings were about gravity and motion. For example, we learned about forces and how they affect motion, Newton's 1's and 2d law of motion, and gravitational interactions. [Constant forward forces, backward forces and constant speed]

I learned
I learned many things. For example I learned what is terminal speed. it is when a free falling object reaches constant speed.

Questions
• Does density affect gravity?
• does shape affect gravity?
• what is newton's 3rd law?

Main Connections
U3C1a2 ⟷ U3C1a5
U3C2 ⟷ purpose   They connect because they
U3C2a7 ⟶ U3C1a7   are all the main Ideas of
U3C2a8 ⟷ U3C1a2   the unit.

Feelings
This process is very confusing in the beginning, but in the end you are able to see the big picture.

TEACHER BENEFITS

Planning

Notebooks provide a structure for teachers to use to outline the conceptual flow of a unit, linking concepts from day to day between lessons. They also allow a teacher to make sure that lessons are complete with a learning cycle that accesses students' prior knowledge, gives them multiple ways to build understanding, and promotes student metacognition. Using interactive notebooks forces a teacher to think about the whole lesson and include all 5 Es.

Classroom Management

All student work is organized in this central location. Moreover, all student thinking is recorded in the same central location, so this makes classroom management of paper a lot easier and less frustrating for both the teacher and the student. (No lost pages and no messy packets!)

Assessment

Assessment is easier—you are assessing all the time, in so many ways, that you can really be in touch with your students. You get an opportunity to see and hear what is going on, and the process allows you to keep a close eye on student misconceptions. Notebooks are the perfect place to give feedback on student learning. Students communicate their understanding through assessments that are incorporated into the notebook pages.

Communication

Notebooks open lines of communication from student to student, student to teacher, student to parent, and parent to teacher. Parents are more easily kept informed as the notebooks clearly show the students did the work, or they didn't. Parents can monitor their child's progress and actually know what their child is learning. Parents can then support the teacher and work as a team to promote their child's success.

I will close by saying once again that I am passionate about using interactive notebooks. Since I have been using this approach to science instruction, I have seen many positive changes in my classroom reflected in the work students do, the questions they ask, and the overall atmosphere. I hope you are inspired to begin using these powerful learning tools.

Resource A

Reproducibles

Interactive Notebook Rubric

10	**"Totally Awesome" (Almost Gross)** 🍎 The writing goes beyond the basic requirements and shows in-depth understanding of concepts. 🍎 The work shows in-depth reflection throughout the learning process. 🍎 Your notebook has all the components expected, including dates and labels on each page. 🍎 All pages are numbered properly with odd numbers on the right and even numbers on the left. 🍎 Right- and left-side work is correctly organized with all criteria. 🍎 The use of color and labeled diagrams enhance understanding. 🍎 The notebook is so tidy it's almost "gross!"
9	**"Awesome"** 🍎 The writing follows the basic requirements, shows understanding of concepts, but does not go beyond. 🍎 The work shows in-depth reflection. 🍎 Your notebook has all the components expected, including dates and labels on each page. 🍎 All pages are numbered properly with odd numbers on the right and even numbers on the left. 🍎 Right- and left-side work is correctly organized with all criteria. 🍎 The notebook has color, and the student uses labeled diagrams. 🍎 A "9" looks much like a "10," but it lacks the "totally" in "awesome."
8	**"Pretty Darn Good"** 🍎 The written work shows a basic understanding of concepts. 🍎 An honest reflection, but limited. 🍎 Your notebook has about 90% of the components expected, with dates and labels. 🍎 All pages are numbered properly with odd numbers on the right and even numbers on the left. 🍎 Right- and left-side work is correctly organized. 🍎 The notebook has some color and diagrams, with a few labels. 🍎 Some requirements are met, but your notebook lacks criteria in all areas.
7	**"Kick It Up a Notch"** 🍎 The written work shows a limited understanding of concepts. 🍎 Limited reflection overall. 🍎 Your notebook has about 80% of the components expected, with dates and labels. 🍎 Most pages are numbered. 🍎 Right- and left-side work is fairly organized, "just so-so." 🍎 The notebook has very little color and hardly any diagrams. 🍎 Notebook requirements are rarely met.
6	**"Better Get Movin'"** 🍎 The written work shows misconceptions and a lack of understanding. 🍎 "Reflection, what reflection?" 🍎 The pages in your notebook are unfinished. 🍎 You tried, but the dates and labels did not make it to the page. 🍎 There are inconsistencies in your right- and left-side entries. 🍎 The notebook is unorganized, and "the dog ate your pages."
5	**"What Were You Thinking?"** 🍎 Hey, you turned in a notebook, but the pages are blank, or they include the class template only. "Maybe you wrote with invisible ink?"

Reproducible 1

Aha Connections Visual Outline

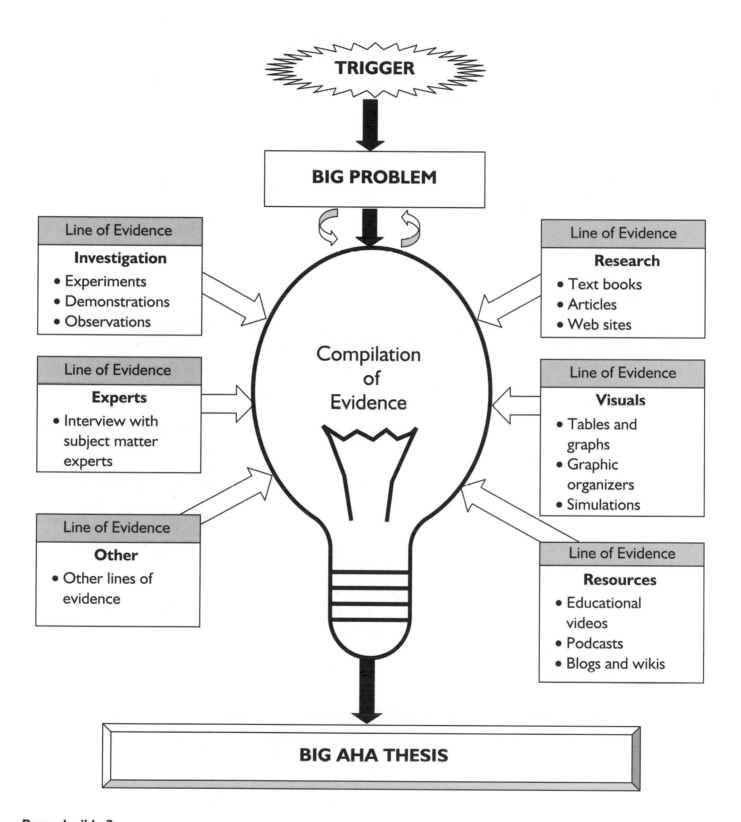

TRIGGER

BIG PROBLEM

Line of Evidence

Investigation

- Experiments
- Demonstrations
- Observations

Line of Evidence

Experts

- Interview with subject matter experts

Line of Evidence

Other

- Other lines of evidence

Compilation of Evidence

Line of Evidence

Research

- Text books
- Articles
- Web sites

Line of Evidence

Visuals

- Tables and graphs
- Graphic organizers
- Simulations

Line of Evidence

Resources

- Educational videos
- Podcasts
- Blogs and wikis

BIG AHA THESIS

Reproducible 2

Words of Wisdom About
the Aha Connections Visual Outline

Scientists gather evidence from many sources, including investigations, research, experts, visuals, and other resources. This evidence often supports and or refutes other lines of evidence. The goal of this approach to immersion and interactive notebooks is to allow students to gather information from many sources in order to critically answer scientific problems.

Trigger

A trigger is a *spark* of interest that leads students to their question or big problem. In order to allow students an opportunity to find this spark, students need to be given time to do observations. (Visual observations, asking questions, reading, watching educational videos, interviewing scientists, etc.) This provides an opportunity for buy in for all students.

Big Problem

Students think about their readings, visual observations, and so on, and start forming questions. These questions are summarized into one big problem or question that students can now investigate.

Lines of Evidence

Students can gather evidence from many sources. The rectangular boxes list these sources of evidence. Often, students of science get their evidence primarily from lab experiments; however, there are other sources that can be used to support or refute evidence found during experimentation. Lines of evidence include but are not limited to investigations, research, consulting experts, visuals, simulations, and other resources.

Compilation of Evidence

Students gather all lines of evidence and find connections or conflicts among pieces of information. As students are compiling this information, they may find that there are holes in their evidence and they need to do more research.

The Aha Thesis

The students take all of the evidence that they have collected and compile it into a formal writing piece. The end result should be a multiparagraph essay with an introductory paragraph, body paragraphs that summarize each line of evidence, and a closing paragraph. Students can use the lines of evidence as stems for writing their big idea thesis.

Why We Keep Interactive Notebooks in Science

To keep an interactive notebook you will need:

➔ An 8 ½" × 11" spiral notebook with at least 70 pages (college ruled is preferred, and *without* perforated pages is best)
➔ Colored pencils, crayons, and highlighters
➔ Tape
➔ A small pair of scissors
➔ A pen and pencil with an eraser

You will be using your interactive notebook in class every day to help you learn new science concepts and to help you make connections to those concepts. Your interactive notebook will also help you organize your thoughts in a fun and creative way.

Left Side—Output *Even numbered pages*	Right Side—Input *Odd numbered pages*
The left side of the notebook is used to show your understanding of the new concepts that you are learning in class. We call this the metacognition, or higher-level thinking, side of your notebook. You will be working with the information from the right, input, side and presenting it in your own way on this left side. We use the left side for . . .	The right side of the notebook is for your facilitated learning. This side is mostly used for the work that you do in class with your teacher and with other classmates. We have a lot of conversations and questions that we try to answer. You will be recording that work on this, right, side of your notebook. We use the right side for . . .
✂ Your questions	✂ Key questions
✂ Brainstorming diagrams	✂ Hypotheses
✂ Making connections	✂ Procedures
✂ Graphing	✂ Labs/Observations
✂ Summary/Conclusions	✂ Data
✂ Applying what you know to the real world/Big Idea	✂ Key words/Notes/Class consensus ideas

Reproducible 4

Interactive Notebook Thinking Processes
(The Thinking Process Students Go Through While Using Their Interactive Notebooks)

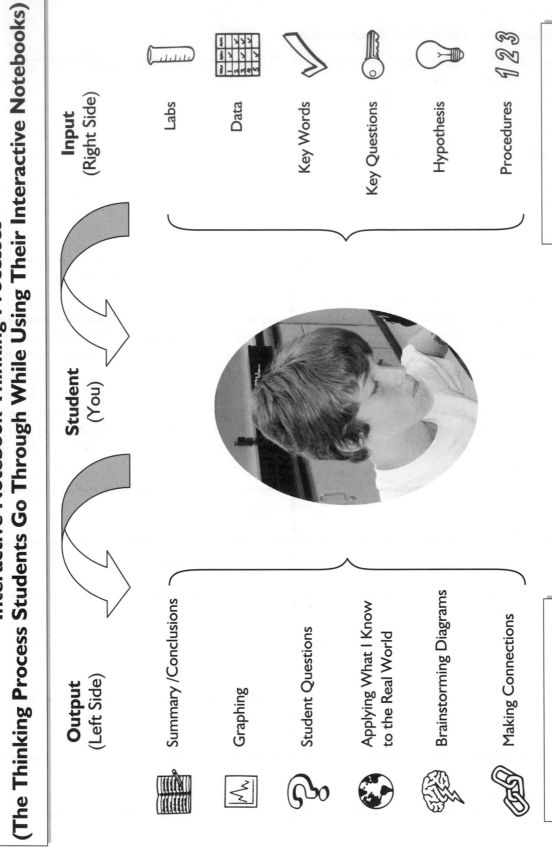

Output
(Left Side)

Summary /Conclusions

Graphing

Student Questions

Applying What I Know
to the Real World

Brainstorming Diagrams

Making Connections

Student
(You)

Input
(Right Side)

Labs

Data

Key Words

Key Questions

Hypothesis

Procedures

Facilitated Learning

Metacognition
(Higher-Level Thinking)

Reproducible 5

Constructing the Aha Connections Pages

The Aha Connections pages are located at the beginning of each new unit in your Interactive Notebook.

First — Two side-by-side pages

Second — In the center, or close to it, write your problem statement or big idea.

e.g., "What is an interaction?"

Third — After each class activity, you will be asked to write a statement that conveys the concept learned.

For example: "Today we learned that you can never obtain an exact value, but you can get very close. Scientists call this 'best value.'"

Fourth
- Take time to share out with a partner!
- Notice trends or connections!
- Use arrows or color to show those trends or connections visually! "Did this lab connect to the Big Aha problem, to another lab, or both?"

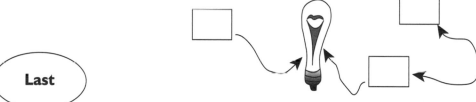

Last — Use these statements as evidence and stems to later write your aha thesis.

Reproducible 6

How to Write an Aha Connections Thesis

What is an aha connections thesis?

It is a thesis paper, generated by you, that addresses the Big Aha or big problem of the unit, using evidence gathered along the way.

1. Let's get started by gathering what you need.

- Go back to the aha connections pages in your interactive notebook.
- Look for the key ideas or concepts you identified from the unit.
- Which lines of evidence best support these key ideas?
- You are now going to use these lines of evidence in your thesis to support your key points.

2. Now, begin by writing your introductory paragraph.

Introductory paragraph:

State the purpose of the unit and the key ideas and concepts learned.

(Hint: That's what you just identified in the four bullets above.)

3. Now you are ready to write the body of your thesis.

Body paragraphs of the thesis (usually three to five paragraphs):

In each of the following paragraphs, give details on one of the key ideas chosen from above.

Use your lines of evidence from your aha connections pages to support your thinking.

(Hint: There is no need to reinvent the wheel; use your own words from the aha connections pages in your interactive notebook.)

4. You are almost there—time to wrap it up.

Final paragraph—conclusion:

- Restate your purpose from the thesis statement.
- Give your thesis the "Hollywood" wrap up.
- Leave a final impression on the reader.

Reproducible 7

___

How to Write a Self-Reflection

You will be expected to write a reflective essay at the end of each unit that shows your in-depth understanding about the work you are doing. Be honest and open in sharing your thoughts and opinions.

Step 1: Count the number of the assignments we have completed for this unit, and record it at the top of your reflection.

Step 2: Choose four pages from this unit that best supported the Big Aha in your unit thesis, two from the left side and two from the right side, and list them on your reflection below the assignment count.

Step 3: You will now be writing three paragraphs.

> **Paragraph 1:** Write specific reasons for why you chose the four assignments that you listed.

> **Paragraph 2:** Explain why these pages best support your unit thesis. Give specific examples.

> **Paragraph 3:** What do these assignments reflect about your skills as a student? For example, you may write that they show that I am organized, I am good at analyzing, I was very thorough, creative, my information was very accurate, I made connections from one assignment to another, and so on. Make sure that you cite specific examples from the pages you listed.

Step 4: This will be Paragraph 4. In this paragraph, you will rate your own notebook. Use the rubric to rate your work as a 10, 9, 8, 7, 6, or 5. How do you think your notebook measures up and why? Use specifics from the rubric, and relate it directly to the pages you listed. (Use examples.)

Step 5: This will be Paragraph 5, the last paragraph of your reflection. Hurray! Answer the following questions:

- What information did you learn that was new to you? Give specific examples.
- How did your notebook help you in this unit? Again, be specific.
- How could you improve your notebook? Please explain.

Please type your final draft, and tape it as a flip page in your interactive notebook as specified by your teacher.

Reproducible 8

Table of Contents for Your Interactive Notebook

Name _____ Unit Title _____

Left Side	Page	Right Side	Page

Total Number of Assignments Completed in this Unit _____

Reproducible 9

Resource B

Crosscurricular Connections

When students are able to make crosscurricular connections and applications of knowledge and skills, powerful learning can result. I have seen many examples in which students were able to carry over skills that we were practicing in science to other classes. Many of the strategies used in notebooks—questioning, summarizing, analyzing, visualizing, pair discussions, evaluating, connecting, interpreting, sharing, and so on—apply to all disciplines and are used to greater and lesser degrees by all teachers. These strategies stand out in the notebooks because they are present on every page every day. Students benefit when we help them become aware that these strategies crossover and realize that they can, for example, apply the same criteria to summary writing in English that they use in science.

In the case of one student, Andy Risser, his math teacher, Mr. Budzynski, and his science teacher, Ms. Marcos, thought that if the graphing strategies that were introduced in science were reinforced in his math class, Andy might have a greater understanding for the concepts that Mr. Budzynski was trying to get his students to grasp. They chose one student because tracking multiple students can become overwhelming, and they felt that the strategies they wanted to focus on would benefit all students in math, even though they were only going to monitor one student. The teacher team chose graphing because the student work that they expected to generate would easily provide evidence of whether the student understood or made the crossover from one content area to another.

In science, the students were taught some basic graphing criteria. The teacher modeled the x and y-axis and pointed out that the IV (independent variable) always goes on the x-axis, and that the DV (dependent variable) always goes on the y-axis. The class discussed what IV and DV are, or how one might identify which should be which in a given experiment. With encouragement from the teacher, the students came up with some prompts to help them identify the IV and DV: "I control . . . , I change . . ." for the IV, and "I have no control, it is what it is" for the DV. They practiced how to set up data tables and deciding which type of graph to use when— which is harder than most people think and requires explicit instruction for students to learn. The main focus of instruction and criteria for success in the science class became the graph title, labels, and summary, which was called the "This Graph Shows . . ." All of this was very similar to what they were already doing in math class. The main difference was the vocabulary and the "This Graph Shows . . ." After their instruction, both teachers felt that the students could follow the basic format but that they had difficulty explaining what the graph represented. The other problem was that the students thought that in science, we do it this way; and in math, we do it that way. A graph is a graph, it doesn't matter what class you are in, but the students repeatedly left the summary and title off in math and just rewrote the title as a summary in science. For example, one student group wrote, "This graph shows that the length of the string on a pendulum makes a difference when it swings back and forth 10 times." A summary that would show more analysis of what was observed would sound something like, "This graph shows that the longer the string, the more time it took for the pendulum to swing back and forth 10 times. I know this because in the graph, the line keeps increasing as the length of the string increases," which, in fact, is what the same group wrote three days later, after rewriting their "This Graph Shows . . ." summary.

Both teachers reinforced this emphasis on analysis in the summary during the month of November. At the end of January, two months later, the math teacher assigned the graphing task in Figure B.1.

Figure B.1   Notice how the task is very basic; there is no mention of titles, IV, DV, labeling, or "This Graph Shows . . ." The students were given a set of numbers and asked to find the best-fit line.

Topic: Biology

Background Information:

Scientists use samples to generalize relationships they observe in nature. The table shows the length and weight of several humpback whales. A long ton is about 2240 pounds.

The Goal: To graph the data and find the Best Fit Line.

The Table

Length (feet)	Weight (long tons)
40	25
42	29
45	34
46	35
50	43
52	45
55	51

An amazing thing happened! From these instructions came Andy's graph, seen in Figure B.2.

Figure B.2 Notice how Andy labeled his x and y-axes, used the proper format for his title, "How does the IV affect the DV," and more important, automatically included his "This Graph shows . . . " summary without the prompt. Not only is it there, it is also beautiful! He explains what you see and uses specific examples to show why you see that. This improvement is boldfaced, black and white, right in front of us.

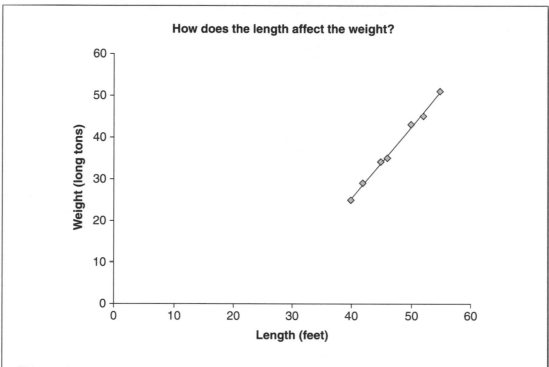

How does the length affect the weight?

This graph shows that the longer the whale measures, the more it weighs. For example, at 40 it weighs 25 long tons, but at 55 feet it weighs 51 long tons. Another example is at 42 feet it weighs 29 long tons but at 45 feet it weighs 34 long tons.

These graphing strategies were reinforced by the teachers in the two classes, and it can be argued that it was the teachers that caused the change. However, I believe it was the interactive notebooks that made the ultimate difference because it was the notebook work that kept the reinforcement fresh in the minds of the students throughout the two months that elapsed in between. Remember, the teachers only focused on graphing crossover in November. After November, there was no mention of the crossover strategies in the math class. However, in science, six separate tasks generated graphs. Students were required to comply with the graphing criteria on all assignments, which they did. Two months later in math class, there was no mention of such criteria. Andy automatically made the connection and crossed over, taking skills from science into math.

Four months later, in May, two students who were struggling with making meaning in math produced the graphs in Figure B.3.

Figure B.3 The students who created this graph and the one on the next page were able to apply the graphing strategies that they learned in science to their math assignment four months later. They did not lose the new knowledge that they had gained; in fact, the explanation of the graph that is represented in the "This Graph Shows . . ." summary is even better than ever. The students show an understanding of the data, and they are able to articulate what they know. The teachers were able to obtain sustainability when it comes to graphing skills.

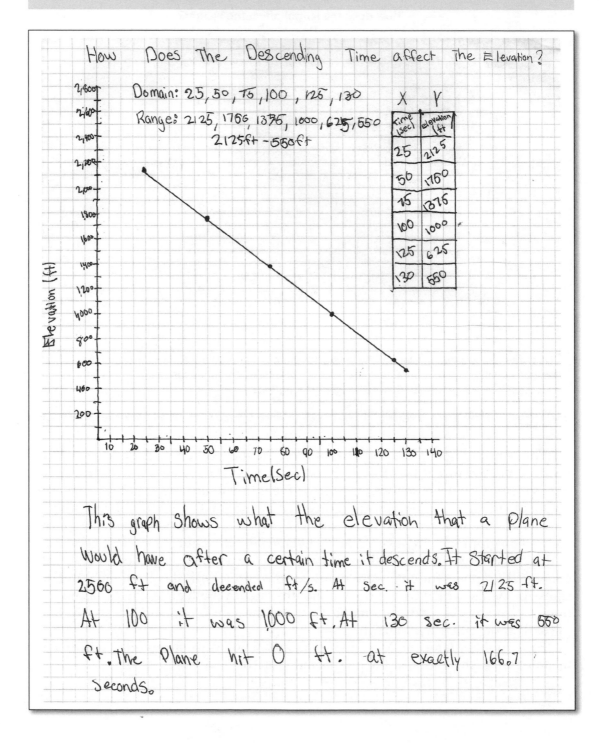

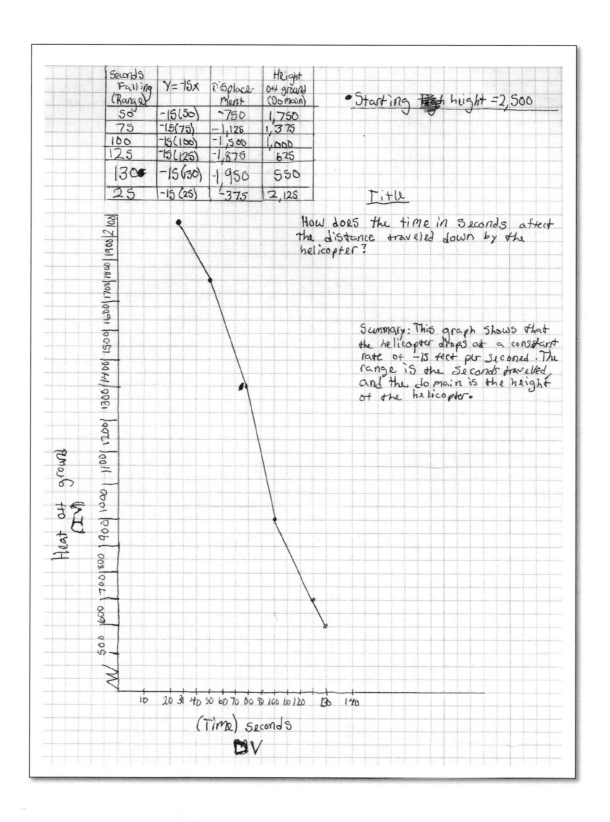

Seconds Falling (Range)	Y = -15x	Displacement	Height off ground (Domain)
50	-15(50)	-750	1,750
75	-15(75)	-1,125	1,375
100	-15(100)	-1,500	1,000
125	-15(125)	-1,875	625
130	-15(130)	-1,950	550
25	-15(25)	-375	2,125

• Starting high hight = 2,500

Title

How does the time in seconds affect the distance traveled down by the helicopter?

Summary: This graph shows that the helicopter drops at a constant rate of -15 feet per seconed. The range is the seconds travelled, and the domain is the height of the helicopter.

Heat off ground (IV)

(Time) seconds

IV

There is a significant difference between the graphs that students generated in October and the graphs that they completed in May. One striking and wonderful result is that when students were asked to generate a graph in math, they incorporated the strategies that they learned in science and used them in a math assignment. The overall graphing skills improved in both classes as well. Each time students were asked to create a graph, they had previous graphs in their notebook to which they could refer. They also had their criteria, which were written in their notebook, to use each time they made a graph. Again, if it weren't together in one place for the student, the connection, the consistency, and the reinforcement of the important habit of referring back to previous learning to build new learning would have been lost. I believe that the notebook is essential for students to make strong connections from one concept to another and for helping students to both consciously and unconsciously crossover the ideas that they learn in one class to another class.

References and Further Reading

Abell, S. K., & Volkmann, M. J. (2006). *Seamless assessment in science: A guide for elementary and middle school teachers.* Arlington, VA: National Science Teachers Association Press.

Amaral, O. M., Garrison, L., & Klentschy, M. (2002, Summer). Helping English learners increase achievement through inquiry-based science instruction. *Bilingual Research Journal, 26*(2), 213–239.

American Association for the Advancement of Science. (1993). *Benchmarks for science literacy.* New York: Oxford University Press.

Black, P., & Wiliam, D. (1998). Inside the black box: Raising standards through classroom assessment. *Phi Delta Kappan, 80*(2), 139–148.

Bybee, R. W. (2002). *Learning science and the science of learning: Science educator's essay collection.* Arlington, VA: National Science Teachers Association Press.

Bybee, R. W., Powell, J. C., & Trowbridge, L. W. (2007). *Teaching secondary school science: Strategies for developing scientific literacy* (9th ed.). Upper Saddle River, NJ: Prentice Hall.

Campbell, B., & Fulton, L. (2003). *Science notebooks.* Portsmouth, NH: Heinemann.

Donovan, M. S., & Bransford, J. D. (2005). *How students learn science in the classroom.* Washington, DC: National Academy Press.

Gilbert, J., & Kotelman, M. (2005, December). Five good reasons to use science notebooks. *Science & Children, 43*(3), 28–32.

Glynn, S., & Muth, D. (1994). Reading and writing to learn science: Achieving scientific literacy. *Journal of Research in Science Teaching, 31*(9), 1057–1073.

Gonzales, P., Williams, T., Jocelyn, L., Roey, S., Kastberg, D., & Brenwald, S. (2008). *Highlights from TIMSS 2007: Mathematics and science achievement of U.S. fourth- and eighth-grade students in an international context.* Washington, DC: National Center for Education Statistics, Institute of Education Sciences, U.S. Department of Education.

Hargrove, T., & Nesbit, C. (2003). *Science notebooks: Tools for increasing achievement across the curriculum.* (ERIC Document Reproduction Service No. ED482720). Retrieved January 10, 2010, from http://www.ericdigests.org/2004-4/notebooks.htm.

Heritage, M. (2010). *Formative assessment: Making it happen in the classroom.* Thousand Oaks, CA: Corwin.

Klentschy, M. P. (2008). *Using science notebooks in elementary classrooms.* Arlington, VA: National Science Teachers Association Press.

Langer, J. A., & Applebee, A. N. (1987). *How writing shapes thinking: A study of teaching and learning.* (NCTE Research Report No. 22). Urbana, IL: National Council of Teachers of English.

Madden, M. (2001, June). *Improving student achievement with interactive notebooks.* Arlington, VA: Arlington County Public Schools.

Magnusson, S. J., & Palincsar, A. S. (2003, April). *A theoretical framework for the development of second hand investigation texts.* Paper presented at the American Educational Research Association Conference, Chicago.

Marzano, R., Pickering, D., & Pollock, J. (2001). *Classroom instruction that works.* Alexandria, VA: Association for Supervision and Curriculum Development.

Michaels, S., O'Connor, C., & Resnick, L. B. (2008). Deliberative discourse idealized and realized: Accountable talk in the classroom and in civic life. *Studies in Philosophy and Education, 27*(4), 283–297.

National Research Council. (1996). *National science education standards.* Washington, DC: National Academy Press.

National Research Council. (1999). *How people learn: Brain, mind, experience and school.* Washington, DC: National Academy Press.

National Research Council. (2000). *Inquiry and the national science education standards: A guide for teaching and learning.* Washington, DC: National Academy Press.

National Research Council. (2001). *Classroom assessment and the national science education standards.* Washington, DC: National Academy Press.

National Research Council. (2005). *How students learn science in the classroom.* Washington, DC: National Academy Press.

Rivard, L., & Straw, S. (2000). The effect of talk and writing on learning science: An exploratory study. *Science Education, 84*(5), 566–593.

Saul, W., Reardon, J., Pearce, C., Dieckman, D., & Neutze, D. (2002). *Science workshop: Reading, writing, and thinking like a scientist* (2nd ed.). Portsmouth, NH: Heinemann.

Swartz, B., & Perkins, D. (1989). *Teaching thinking: Issues and approaches.* Pacific Grove, CA: Midwest.

Wallis, C. (2006, December 10). How to bring our schools out of the 20th century. *TIME Magazine.*

White, B., & Fredrickson, J. (1998). Inquiry, modeling, and metacognition: Making science accessible to all students. *Cognition and Instruction, 16*(1), 42–56.

Wiggins, G., & McTighe, J. (1998). *Understanding by design.* Alexandria, VA: Association for Supervision and Curriculum Development.

Young, J. (2003, January). Science interactive notebooks in the classroom. *Science Scope, 26*(4), 44–47.

Index

CORWIN

A SAGE Company

The Corwin logo—a raven striding across an open book—represents the union of courage and learning. Corwin is committed to improving education for all learners by publishing books and other professional development resources for those serving the field of PreK–12 education. By providing practical, hands-on materials, Corwin continues to carry out the promise of its motto: **"Helping Educators Do Their Work Better."**